JACK BAUER'S
HAVING A BAD DAY

An Unauthorized Investigation
of Faith in 24: Season 1

JACK BAUER'S
HAVING A BAD DAY

TIM

WESEMANN

LIFE JOURNEY®
Bringing Home the Message for Life

COOK COMMUNICATIONS MINISTRIES
Colorado Springs, Colorado • Paris, Ontario
KINGSWAY COMMUNICATIONS LTD
Eastbourne, England

This book is a critical commentary on the religious themes found in the television show *24*. This book has not been approved, licensed, endorsed, or sponsored by Twentieth Century Fox and is in no way associated with any entity involved in creating or producing the television series *24*.

Life Journey® is an imprint of
Cook Communications Ministries, Colorado Springs, CO 80918
Cook Communications, Paris, Ontario
Kingsway Communications, Eastbourne, England

JACK BAUER'S HAVING A BAD DAY
© 2006 Tim Wesemann

Cover Design: Charles Brock, The DesignWorks Group, Inc.
Cover Photo: © iStock

First Printing, 2006
Printed in Canada

1 2 3 4 5 6 7 8 9 10 Printing/Year 10 09 08 07 06

Unless otherwise noted, Scripture quotations are taken from the *Holy Bible, New International Version*®. *NIV*®. Copyright © 1973, 1978, 1984 by International Bible Society. Used by permission of Zondervan. All rights reserved. Scripture quotations marked MSG are taken from *THE MESSAGE*. Copyright © by Eugene H. Peterson 1993, 1994, 1995, 1996, 2000, 2001, 2002. Used by permission of NavPress Publishing Group; and NIrV are taken from the *HOLY BIBLE, NEW INTERNATIONAL READER'S VERSION*®. Copyright © 1996, 1998 International Bible Society. All rights reserved throughout the world. Used by permission of International Bible Society. Italics in Scripture quotations have been added by the author for emphasis.

ISBN-13: 978-0-7814-4384-5
ISBN-10: 0-7814-4384-9

LCCN: 2006929214

For Benjamin,
who introduced our family to 24.
And for Dean,
who helped me recognize faith truths all around me—
24 hours a day.

Contents

Acknowledgments

I'm so thankful that the Lord chose to gift me with this writing opportunity and for the living gifts with which he surrounds me as I write.

Mike Nappa—Thank you for this opportunity and for causing me to grow and grow as a riter, I mean writer. I'm extremely grateful that you challenged and encouraged me to take my writing to the next level.

The entire Cook team—I'm grateful for your hard work in bringing this project to fruition. Special thanks to Diane for coordinating this investigation of faith.

Steve Laube—Thank you for jumping in and handling those small and large details. I'm thankful you have those gifts.

Chiara, Christopher, Sarah, and Benjamin—Even when I seemed glued to the computer, I was really stuck on you! Thank you for allowing me the time to write for him. In Christ's love you'll find my love for you.

Judy Rehmer—The gifts of your time, editing, and encouragement have more than caught the eye of our Savior. He has blessed you, and you have been a true blessing to me and my writing ministry. Thank you.

My family outside the walls of my home—Thank you for your loving support. Mom and Dad—our Savior will pass on my love and thanks.

My friends, prayer partners, and encouragers—This book became a reality because you helped carry this work before God's throne of grace. Thanks to Dennis and Venus, Don Clair, Kay, Nathan, Kenda, Amy, Matt, and Richard for their contributions, as well as the entire body of encouragers at Faith and CTA.

Introduction

RIGHT NOW, TERRORISTS ARE PLOTTING TO
ASSASSINATE A PRESIDENTIAL CANDIDATE, MY
WIFE AND DAUGHTER ARE IN TROUBLE, AND
PEOPLE THAT I WORK WITH MAY BE INVOLVED
IN BOTH. I'M FEDERAL AGENT JACK BAUER—
THIS IS THE LONGEST DAY OF MY LIFE.

—JACK BAUER
(PORTRAYED BY KIEFER SUTHERLAND),
FROM THE HIT TV SHOW 24

>>The clock is ticking ...

If you're like me, you probably watch a little television. If you're like the tens of millions of people who are also like me, the television you watch each week probably includes an hour or so of the heart-pounding, action-suspense drama 24. You also know that Jack Bauer, its lead character, is having a bad day ... but that's a good thing, for us!

It's a good thing because incidents from Jack's adrenaline-charged life reveal twenty-four unexpected truths about faith in God, and we can benefit from discovering and exploring those truths. I like to call those unexpected truth moments "adrenaline for the soul" because they do for my faith life what the pulse-raising drama of 24 does for my entertainment life. They get me pumped up and excited about what's to come next!

Now, before I go on, I suspect this would be a good time to offer a disclaimer of sorts, as there are a few things you should know before reading this book.

First, I am a Christian. In fact, I am a former pastor and even hold one of those fancy master of divinity degrees from seminary. Take that for what it's worth to you. I just thought you should know up front.

Second, I'm a fan of heart-pounding, action-suspense drama on television. (Big surprise, huh?)

Third, although *24* is one of my favorite shows, it is definitely *not* intended to be a religious one. The sometimes-graphic content and occasional profanity incorporated into the show's scripts are proof enough of that. In fact, my guess is that the show's creators would be very surprised to hear about anyone drawing religious truth from the characters, scenes, and situations of their show.

But that leads me to the fourth thing I want to tell you. Absurd as it may seem, *24* has been a catalyst for my spiritual growth. Watching this show with my Christian worldview, I couldn't help but see the truths of Scripture revealing themselves in the unfolding events of its fictional federal agent, Jack Bauer, and those who surround him. Whether they intended to do so or not, the creators of *24 have* embedded unexpected lessons about a life of faith in the captivating moments of their weekly drama. (Gosh, they're more talented than even they think they are!)

24: Season One Key Players	
Jack Bauer	Heads the Los Angeles Counter Terrorism Unit (CTU)
Teri Bauer	Jack's wife
Kimberly (Kim) Bauer	Jack and Teri's teenage daughter
Senator David Palmer	Presidential candidate
Sherry Palmer	David's wife
Nicole and Keith Palmer	David and Sherry's daughter and son
Nina Myers	Jack's friend and CTU agent
Tony Almeida	CTU agent
Jamey Farrell	CTU computer expert
Richard Walsh	CTU Superior
George Mason	CTU District Agent
Ryan Chappelle	CTU Regional Director
Andre and Alexis Drazen	Serbian brothers
Victor Drazen	Father of Andre and Alexis
Ira Gaines	Works for Drazen
Mandy and Bridget	Work for Ira Gaines
Martin Belkin	Photographer
Dan and Rick	Kidnappers; Gaines' thugs
Janet York	Friend of Kimberly Bauer
Kevin Carroll, alias Alan York	Works for Gaines and Drazen brothers

And if you think about it, Jack Bauer's life in the "real time" of our TV sets mirrors many aspects of Jesus' real life on earth. In fact, in my "sanctified imagination," I expect that some days his words could have been ...

> Right now, terrorists are plotting to assassinate me, my followers are in trouble, and my handpicked disciples may be involved in both. I am the promised Messiah, Jesus Christ—this is the longest day of my life.

What about events in the real time of your life and mine? I suspect that many days you and I both (if we were TV drama scriptwriters, of course) might say these familiar words ...

> Right now, my headache's killing me, my family has all sorts of troubles, and my hectic schedule plays a part in both. I am [insert your name here]—this is the longest day of my life.

So, in *Jack Bauer's Having a Bad Day* I want to investigate twenty-four unexpected faith truths, using a bridge point from each of the twenty-four episodes from the first season of the hit TV show *24*. Using the vivid, powerful drama of a specific scene from each episode we will embark on an engaging exploration of the truth of God relative to core faith concepts, and we will apply our findings to events in the very real time of our days.

Okay, that was the former seminarian in me coming out. Let me say it another way: Let's take a little time right now to relive a few exciting moments from the first season of *24*—and let's learn a little bit more about what it means to live a life of faith in God in the process.

All right, then.

>>The clock is ticking ...

Ready or not, here we go!

Life on the Run Isn't a Walk in the Park

God! God!
I am running to you for dear life;
the chase is wild.
If they catch me, I'm finished:
ripped to shreds by foes fierce as lions,
dragged into the forest and left
unlooked for, unremembered.
—King David
Psalm 7:1–2 (MSG)

I got her password— LIFESUCKS—one word.

—Jack Bauer, trying to track down his runaway daughter by accessing her e-mail account

>>I was thinking we should try to remember what it was like when we were kids, you know?
>>It's a different ... world now, Jack.
—Phone conversation between Jack and Teri Bauer after their daughter sneaks out for the night

We can't place an ear on the strategist's head to listen in on his thoughts, but the intense gleam in his eyes tells his story as he masterminds his next line of attack. He has *that* look. A look that oozes confidence. His words work the room ... the deep, smooth tone of his voice—one any Hollywood voice-over talent would kill for. His handsomely rugged face and toned body cause women to take more than a second glance. Below that surface, Jack Bauer is a relentless tactician, deftly initiating spare options anytime any plan fails. And, although we don't have a medical report to substantiate it, his DNA strands clearly indicate he's all about success and has an undeniable drive to protect. Two small genetic strands, compassion and devotion, intertwine with the rest to embody all that is Jack Bauer.

>>The clock is ticking ...

>>You're in trouble ...

Trouble means little in a strategic chess match between father and teenage daughter. Trouble in this game is nothing compared to the checkmate standoffs soon to challenge this family.

Jack's daughter, Kim, leans back in her chair, opposite her dad, confident that her chess moves will soon bring down her father, the superstrategist. Surrounded by the serenity of their suburban-looking home, they enjoy a quiet game until the intensity level rises ever so slightly as the scent of checkmate fills the air.

>>You're in trouble, Dad.

>>Really?

Is Kim Bauer a modern-day prophetess in a pink bathrobe? Her loaded remark will soon blow up in her face as she plays the role of a pawn in a lethal match of real-life checkmate.

>>You're in trouble, Dad.

Jack chooses to play his parental checkmate move next, noting that the ticking clock has passed midnight. Kim's half smile and refusal to put up a fight mean she'll give her dad this little escape because she knows it will give her the bigger victory she really wants in just a few more ticks of the minute hand. She leans down, sharing a good-night kiss and loving word with her dad before passing through the kitchen and sharing an *attitude* with her mom—without a thought of a kiss or loving words.

Strategically she pits dad against mom, blaming Teri for a recent-but-short separation between them. She senses success as the intensity level climbs a few notches.

Kim meanders down the hall to her bedroom, but as soon as she crosses its threshold she shifts into high gear. She closes her door, cranks up her stereo, discards the bathrobe that hides an outfit a mall rat might pick up for a night out, and climbs out her window to a waiting friend's nearby car. Her life moves from calm to chaos in less than five minutes. The intensity gauge climbs even more.

>>Now who's in trouble, Kim?

The window escape sets the plan in motion. The waiting SUV's engine revs softly outside as Kim sprints toward it. Two high school girls. One SUV. Hopefully a pair of oblivious parents. And one plan: hook up with two guys.

Unfortunately, as the SUV peels out down the street, Kim's once-oblivious parents realize the obvious.

Kim snuck out. The *why?* and *where to?* questions go unanswered as the intensity needle skips a few notches on its way to dangerous levels.

Teri and Jack quickly search Kim's room, looking for evidence of where she might have gone. The search party is interrupted unexpectedly when the sound of Jack's cell phone calls him into an immediate high-level security meeting at the Los Angeles Counter Terrorism Unit (CTU), where he's director.

>>No! Not now. Our daughter's in trouble.

Jack knows he has to pull out of this family crisis without Teri's backing ... like all too often before ... as work moves the CTU director into a *check* position. Teri is tired of Jack's loyalty to CTU taking precedence over their family.

>>You're in trouble, Dad.

So are you, Kim. So is Teri. And so is Senator Palmer, as we'll soon find out.

All of us are about to experience the longest day of our lives.

>>The clock is ticking ...

No longer a risk-taking teen like Kimberly, my friend Randy Rogers has lived the last twenty years on the run. During those years, Randy has traveled over 33,000 miles. You see, twenty years ago he made a commitment to run *at least* one mile a day. Randy hasn't missed a day. And rarely does he run only one mile. His daily average is 4.7 miles.

Thirty-three thousand miles. Eleven full marathons. Through rain, sleet, heat, ice—even minus-thirty-degree temperatures—he runs. That's no walk (or run, in his case) in the park.

> **"To those of us in the middle of a marathon, running from people or things, twenty-four hours of freedom sounds good about now."**

Even with Randy's influence, I'm not a runner. Well, sometimes I am, I guess. I run errands. In fact, last Tuesday my errand running (in my car, that is) took me 26.2 miles around town. That's a marathon of sorts. At times, I've even lived on the run.

I've tried to outrun bills that piled up. Confused about decisions, I've spent time running aimlessly, wondering what to do. When I couldn't handle responsibilities, I ran to find a place to hide. Have you been there too? I'm not running alone, am I?

If you care to spill the beans, maybe you've found yourself

- moving continually, keeping busy so you don't have to deal with a tense relationship at home;
- sprinting toward every other get-rich-quick scheme, hoping those riches quickly catch up with your debt;
- darting away from a deep-seated childhood idea that you have to be perfect and expect perfection, nothing less;

- hustling to prove you can succeed, driven by someone's expectation that you'll fail;
- running for your life, searching desperately for the happiness that eludes you.

If none of those situations fit the bill, there's always room for a personal write-in vote. To those of us in the middle of a marathon, running from people or things, twenty-four hours of freedom sounds good about now. A personal "long day's night" may have just passed its week, month, or year marker. In truth, we're a lot like Jack Bauer, caught up in adrenaline-pounding circumstances, fearful for the safety of our loved ones, and not sure who to trust or where to go for help.

>> HISTORICALLY, THE LONGEST DAY TOOK PLACE IN SEPTEMBER OF 1752, WHEN THE WORLD CHANGED FROM THE JULIAN CALENDAR TO THE GREGORIAN CALENDAR. PEOPLE WENT TO BED ON SEPTEMBER 2; THEY WOKE UP ON SEPTEMBER 14.

In the opening episode of 24's first season, Kim attempts to run from childhood into adulthood. She's disillusioned and unhappy at home—something summed up in her Internet password: "LIFESUCKS."

Jack and Teri have to keep moving forward too, to get past previous marital problems that separated them briefly. Senator Palmer—the leading candidate in the race for the presidency—isn't running *away* from something. He's rushing forward to take a stand for the truth on his way to the highest office in the land. Life on the run certainly isn't a walk in the park for *any* of these players! And it's often not a rosy experience for you and me either. *24*'s interesting phenomenon often mirrors our lives; we are always running.

Elijah can relate. The Old Testament prophet Elijah knows exactly what it means to be on the run for one's life. He lives it. "Elijah was afraid and ran for his life" (1 Kings 19:3). Like many of

> **"If Kimberly Bauer's Internet password is 'LIFESUCKS,' Elijah's password could be 'LIFESTINKETH'!"**

the characters in *24*, he is chased and terrorized. The queen wants him dead, and Elijah feels like a lone pawn trying to protect his King.

If Kimberly Bauer's Internet password is "LIFESUCKS," Elijah's password could be "LIFESTINKETH"!

When Queen Jezebel discovers he's executed her false prophets, she sends word to Elijah that within twenty-four hours she will have him assassinated as well (see 1 Kings 19).

Twenty-four hours. (Has a familiar ring to it, doesn't it?) The clock is ticking for Elijah (or more appropriately, the shadows on the sundial are moving ...).

Walk the Talk, Elijah!

But instead of trusting God, Elijah decides to play it solo and makes an ill-advised move on his own. His faith begins to waver. His focus veers from heaven to himself. His God-born confidence shrivels. Fear moves in, and Elijah the prophet becomes just another man running for his life.

>>Wake up, Elijah, you're God's man, and you want to give up? Will *the real* Elijah please come forward?

>>**WE'RE FICKLE WHEN IT COMES TO FAITH. WE WAVER. AT THE FIRST SIGN OF TROUBLE, WE ASSUME GOD'S FORGOTTEN US.**

I'm havin' a good time dissin' ol' Elijah, until I realize that *is* the real Elijah. And sadly, that scenario is *my* real-life story too. (I'm betting it's probably yours, as well.) We're fickle when it comes to faith. We waver. At the first sign of trouble, we assume God's forgotten us. We find ourselves facing the hardships of life, the consequences of bad decisions, and the attacks of evil people; and instead of trusting God, we do what comes naturally.

We run.

Just like Kim Bauer. Just like Jack and Teri Bauer.

Just like Elijah ... who had a Jack Bauer kind of bad day ... but that can be a good thing for us as God uses that prophet's story to enlighten and encourage us with a faith truth.

Wait! Before you prepare to read a sermon on running to God instead of running away from him, sit tight. That's not the truth to take away from Elijah's life—or ours. You see, the exhausted and depressed Elijah falls asleep, hoping he'll never wake up. But an angel of the Lord provides him food and drink along with his siesta (which becomes a power nap as through it God injects Elijah with his power). The angel wakes Elijah and says, "Get up and eat, for the journey is too much for you" (v. 7).

Through the miraculous angelic visit, God gives Elijah sustenance for the hard journey ahead. "Strengthened by that food, [Elijah] traveled forty days and forty nights until he reached Horeb, the mountain of God" (v. 8).

Jezebel's twenty-four-hour death threat evaporates over the next forty days. Oh, she still wants

"God proves worthy of Elijah's trust ..."

to kill him, make no mistake. But God gets involved and makes it impossible for the evil queen to lay a hand on his chosen prophet.

In short, God proves worthy of Elijah's trust—even when Elijah finds himself on the run, frightened to the heart in the face of danger. We've been down that road. We can't run the distance on our own. But it's not too much for our Savior to handle.

> **"We can't run the distance on our own. But it's not too much for our Savior to handle."**

Nothing is.

Jesus Christ even defeated the terrorist of terrorists, Satan—and he did it with two hands nailed to a cross! Interestingly, that victory happened on a day we don't refer to as *bad*, but rather as *good*—Good Friday.

It's no walk in the park when you live on the run.

>>You're in trouble ...

But that's okay for you and me, friend, because God runs with us, and we know he deserves our *trust*.

FAITH TRUTH #2
Trust Is a Must

>>Jack, listen to me. Take this card, and give it to Jamey. Baylor said that we could trust her ... she'll match it to a computer. Find the computer, you've got the dirty agent.
—Richard Walsh with keycard in hand, just prior to receiving a fatal gunshot wound

Those who know your name
will trust in you,
for you, LORD, have never forsaken
those who seek you.
—Psalm 9:10

I set it up wrong. We were sitting ducks. I'm sorry to put you through this, Jack.

Don't you ever say that to me. You of all people. I owe you my life.

—*Richard Walsh and Jack Bauer, as Walsh sits injured while Jack tends to his gunshot wound*

>>Jack stares in disbelief at the name
on the computer screen.

The elevator doors open, breaking the silence in the empty corridor. Agent Walsh steps out and continues confidently down the hall, his expression resolute. The click of each step pierces the silence and echoes off the empty walls. Suddenly, like in a scene from a suspense movie, Agent Scott Baylor appears from somewhere in the dimly lit recesses of the hall. His body language and rapid-fire words confirm his trust meter sits on zero. With beads of sweat covering his face, Baylor drills his superior, "Did anyone see you come in? You sure you weren't followed?" An attempt to calm him, Walsh's response is met instead with more distrust and anxiety. Desperate to wash his hands of what he uncovered, Baylor hands Walsh a keycard containing confidential files referencing Senator Palmer—an indictment of a mole within the agency.

With the agents' bodies silhouetted in the hallway, silence immediately turns to pandemonium as bullets fly down the corridor, one killing Baylor instantly. Another bullet carves a notch in Walsh's left forearm. Wounded, he narrowly escapes to the roof where he calls Jack to rescue him from what could be their own agents turned against them. Walsh insists that Jack not call anyone else. He doesn't know who to trust.

Jack wastes no time in rushing to Walsh's aid. During the attempt to escape the building, the two agents engage in a shootout with the unknown intruders. Running toward Jack's car and freedom, Walsh is struck by a bullet. Bloodied and lying powerless on the ground, Walsh instructs, "Jack, listen to me. Take this card and give it to Jamey. Baylor said that we could trust her ... she'll match it to a computer. Find the computer, and you've got the dirty agent." Walsh tosses Jack the keycard, and two shots ring out. Walsh grimaces in pain just before his body falls limp on the concrete pavement.

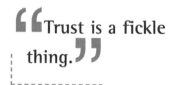
"Trust is a fickle thing."

Realizing there's nothing he can do for Walsh and that his own life is in danger, Jack retreats to his SUV and races down the road to freedom.

Stopping to catch his breath—and the dirty agent—Jack sends Jamey the card information from his car's computer. She decodes the encryption and sends the information back to Jack.

>>Jack stares in disbelief at the name on the computer screen.

Trust is a fickle thing. Or maybe I'm fickle about trust. Jack Bauer doesn't have that problem. He *can't* trust anyone.

I taught my children not to talk to strangers, to choose friends wisely. Wait a minute. I *also* encouraged them to compassionately find ways to help others, get involved in the church's homeless ministry, and participate in mission trips where they'd be surrounded by strangers. No wonder they look confused (handsome and beautiful, but confused).

To trust or not to trust? That is the question. I look in the mirror and realize that half the time I can't even trust the person looking back at me.

Peter, Mary, and Mark intrigue me when it comes to learning about trust. (Peter, Paul, and Mary used to intrigue me when it came to folk music, but that's another story.) Let's start with Peter.

The wind blows ruthlessly through the mostly empty corridor of the Sea of Galilee. His expression resolute, disciple Simon Peter steps out of the wind-tossed boat, places his feet *on* the water, and begins to put one foot in front of the other. Soon the violent wind and churning water become a distraction. While the wind and the waves justify the sudden fear and doubt that overcome him, a sinking feeling overcomes him too. His trust level plummeting as rapidly as his body into the water, Peter cries out, "Lord, save me!" Immediately, the Master reaches out his hand and rescues the waterlogged disciple, whose faith sank from trust to doubt in nothing flat when he took his eyes off Jesus (see Matt. 14:22–33).

> **""I look in the mirror and realize that half the time I can't even trust the person looking back at me.""**

This disarming visual takes me back to my days as a whitewater canoe guide in the North Carolina mountains. The trip climaxed with the running of the Cap'n Crunch rapid. If the paddlers didn't catch the eddy at the end of the rapid, their canoes would slam into a huge rock wall—Cap'n Crunch. One memorable father-son duo barely made it into the rapid when they capsized. Panicking, the father flung his arms, reaching for a tree limb hanging over the river. Instead of grabbing a limb or the rope I threw out, in his flailing panic, he grabbed his own left arm with his right hand!

While the man's mistake was somewhat humorous for the river, it was not the least bit uncommon for the Sea of Life. I don't know about you, but I'm always trying to save myself. How often I hold on to myself, my stubborn ways, and my selfish thoughts when I sink to distrust of the Savior who holds out his hand to rescue me. O *me* of little faith! I have so much to learn and so much trust to invest in the sure hands of Jesus—his hands once pinned to a cross-shaped tree. Only he

>>0 ME OF LITTLE FAITH!

could compassionately and miraculously reach down and save us while at the same time he hung from a cross! No doubt about it, we can trust those hands and echo Peter's thoughts and Jack Bauer's words as we say to our Savior, "I owe you my life."

Mary, too, knew about life. So did her sister, Martha. They also knew about death. They knew whom to trust, whom to call on. They sent word to Jesus, informing him their brother, his friend Lazarus, lay sick. Jesus listened and sat tight. The disciples scratched their heads, confused. By the time Jesus arrived on the scene Lazarus had been buried four days.

I'm curious how Mary and Martha dealt with things during those four days. Did they think or sink? Did they trust Jesus, thinking he would intervene in some way or, in Simon Peter style, did they take their eyes off him? I think the answer is probably both. The first thing both M & M ladies said upon seeing Jesus was, "Lord, if you'd been here, my brother would not have died" (John 11:21, 32). If I had lived in their sandals (which would look pretty silly, now that I think of it), I could easily have heard myself scolding Jesus. "I trusted you, Lord—that's why I

> **"It's so easy to blame God for the bad stuff."**

sent for you! Isn't that what you wanted? But look, do you see my brother? No! That's because he's dead and gone. You let me down—big-time."

It's so easy to blame God for the bad stuff. Drunk drivers run into telephone poles and are killed. The survivoring friends and family blame God. We invest in the hottest new stock option, knowing full well its value could either soar or hit the toilet, and when it does the latter we look heavenward and shake our fists at God—for what? Creating Wall

Street? We treat others with distrust, anger, or plain ol' meanness, and when our relationships with them go south, even the directionally challenged among us run to Jerusalem to hurl our anger at the cross of Jesus.

> **"I sucked up his cards, pictures, and magazine covers faster than a Hoover with ADHD."**

Mary and Martha turned from questioning the Messiah and stepped out with God's glory-strength kind of trust that turns water into a walkway. "But I know that even now God will give you whatever you ask" (John 11:22). With that, the Resurrection and the Life brought Lazarus back to life. But before he did, Jesus looked at the grieving sisters and said,

> "Didn't I tell you that if you believed, you would see the glory of God?"
>
> Then ... Jesus raised his eyes to heaven and prayed, "Father, I'm grateful that you have listened to me. I know you always do listen, but on account of this crowd standing here I've spoken so that they might believe that you sent me." (John 11:40–42 MSG)

Jesus desired their full trust.

Jesus desires our full trust.

St. Louis Cardinals power hitter Mark McGwire had a look of great resolve each time he eyed his opponent sixty and a half feet away. Mark wrote the good news according to the boys of summer—specifically in 1998. I invested a lot in Mark that season. I sucked up his cards, pictures, and magazine covers faster than a Hoover with ADHD. Yes, that was me in the crowd—acting like a kid—when he broke *the* record.

I trusted Mark's bat, his muscles, and his dedication to the game. I trusted his memorabilia would one day pay for my children's college educations and the memories would one day keep my grandchildren standing in awe of their grandpa and his incredible stories.

Then along came the controversy—it started with an *S* and ended in *teroids*. Suddenly, it was a whole new ball game. I know (at least at the time of this writing) Mark hasn't admitted using them, but the public perceives he did and is disillusioned. Even though that assumption isn't fair, the inference taints the memorabilia and memories. "Never again!" I told myself. "They're just ball players."

I realize Mark has no clue who I am, while many of you holding this book wrestle with distrust in much more significant ways as it gnaws at your heart this very moment. In my insignificance, I kept going to games and passed my enjoyment of baseball on to my children. But I've reined in my trust and turned it into an enjoyable hobby. Well, I tried. Then another power hitter, Albert Pujols, showed up on the scene ... But hear me out—I'm not putting my trust in him—it's just a hobby. That's all. Really! ... You don't trust me, do you?

> **❝❝I'd rather take a risk in trusting than live with constant distrust and fear.❞❞**

I've been told I trust too many people, too easily. I'm not naive, just trusting. Many people have taken advantage of my trustfulness, I know. But I'd rather take a risk in trusting than live with constant distrust and fear. I'm striving to trust in a Christlike way, mixing intelligence with love.

I want to have the apostle Paul's contentment—no matter what the situation. My life often sings, "I am trusting me, Tim Wesemann, trusting only me" instead of, "I am trusting THEE, Lord Jesus, trusting ONLY Thee." I want to wallow—be covered from head to foot—in the contenting and challenging message of Proverbs 3:5–6 (MSG):

> Trust God from the bottom of your heart;
> don't try to figure out everything on your own.

Listen for God's voice in everything you do, every-
    where you go;
he's the one who will keep you on track.

> **"Trust in Jesus Christ is a must for healthy, joyful living."**

My hope is that Mary and I can stand together (even in the face of death) and say, "We trusted you, Jesus—even though things didn't turn out like we thought they should or would." I pray Simon Peter will teach me to walk trustingly where others dare to tread, relying on the saving handouts of my Savior. And although I can't speak for Mark, I can speak for myself. Some people have placed me on a pedestal, only to have me let them down, only to learn that my place—our place—for real living is at the feet of the forgiving, graceful Savior whom we can always trust for second chances.

Then there's Jack Bauer, whose world leaves little room for trust. He teaches me to be cautious and beware because an enemy—often more than one—lurks in the darkness, waiting for just the right time to shoot me down. Yet I won't allow myself to live in constant fear. Trust in Jesus Christ is a must for healthy, joyful living.

Like Richard Walsh, we lie powerless at the feet of the one we trust to save us. But this time the dialogue between the weak and the strong is reversed. Our story's Savior empathizes with our living in the mess of sin and an untrusting world. And we, the powerless ones, respond with the words of Jack Bauer, "I owe you my life."

FAITH TRUTH #3
Self-Serve Lines Serve Little Purpose

nar·cis·sism (när′sĭ-sĭz′əm) n.:
Excessive love or admiration of oneself.
The attribute of the human psyche characterized by
admiration of oneself but within normal limits.

—The American Heritage Dictionary of the English
Language, Fourth Edition

That is what the Son of Man
has done:
He came to serve, not to be served—
and then to give away his life
in exchange for many who are
held hostage.
—Mark 10:45 (MSG)

>>Mandy: Money is the *only* thing that these people care about.
>>Bridget: Let's do it anyway. You know he can't hurt us. *Nobody* can hurt us ... One million for you. One million for me. Don't you like the way that suunds?

Ira Gaines can't believe what he's hearing. Drazen, his boss, will probably take it out on him. But he has no choice. He needs Martin Belkin's ID in order to move forward with the Palmer assassination. He *must* give in to their demands. Martin Belkin, an influential photographer, has clearance to attend a photo op for David Palmer. His Belkin impersonator needs that ID.

Mandy and Bridget masterminded the stealing of the ID and the explosion that killed Belkin as well as all the other passengers aboard the plane he was on, and now they hold the ID as a bargaining chip. They want another million; at least that's Bridget's plan. She has hidden the ID. But there's no hiding her greed.

Mandy knows how these people operate. You don't mess with them.

Bridget knows Gaines can't move without the ID. She knows those behind the scheme have the cash to meet her demand for double the money. She attempts to share her greed and a drug fix with Mandy, tempting her with, "Another million dollars doesn't mean anything to these people."

Mandy disagrees, "You're wrong. Money is the *only* thing these people care about." Bridget couldn't care less. She's high on self-indulgence and seduces Mandy with her words, insisting no one can hurt them. They've got it made in the self-serve line at Drazen and Gaines' ATM. Life is good in Narcissism-land ... especially with an extra million bucks in their hands.

Life is also good with twenty items or less in my cart at my neighborhood grocery store. When I was young, the checkout clerk/bagger's job seemed like the coolest job in the world (next to playing for the Cardinals). The baseball gig never worked out (I'm as shocked as you), but God gave me a taste of life as a grocery checker with the invention of self-serve checkout lines. Have you experienced them? You roll your cart next to a computer and enter the necessary information on the screen. Next—and this is the really cool part—you get to scan the items you bought, and the computer actually talks to you. The fun doesn't stop there. You also get to bag your own purchases. Then, of course, you get to pay for the items, *but* there's no extra charge for the thrill of that self-serve pleasure.

I'm easily amused, and you, you're thinking, "This guy needs a life." And you're right. But that is just the point of this faith truth. *I need a life. You need a life.* And there's a real life to be had out there—one that doesn't have self-serve lines that possibly create exaggerated pride.

Even if you've never heard about those fancy grocery store self-serve lines, I bet you've heard some of *these* self-serve lines:

- "I don't care whether you agree; this is what we're doing."
- "I can't believe how many hours I put into this report. Corporate had better notice."
- "I know we can't afford it, but it's gonna be mine."
- "I deserve this, and if I don't get it, I'm out of here."
- "And just what do *I* get out of this?"
- "Forget it! What have you ever done for me?"

Have you bagged up any of these items (or similar ones)? I've occasionally bagged a few favorites. And after bagging them, of course, I've paid their price: broken relationships, broken reputation, broken respect, broken faith (someone else's, if not my own). Guess I'm not a very good bagger; I always break things.

Our Servant Savior knows nothing about self-serving lines, nor does he want us to hang around them. Rather, check out some of these items he bags up for us in the Bread of Life aisle:

You're blessed when you're content with just who you are—no more, no less. That's the moment you find yourselves proud owners of everything that can't be bought. (Matt. 5:5 MSG)

Really! There's no such thing as self-rescue,
pulling yourself up by your bootstraps.
The cost of rescue is beyond our means.
(Ps. 49:7–8 MSG)

Watch out! Be on your guard against wanting to have more and more things. Life is not made up of how much a person has. (Luke 12:15 NIrV)

> **"Our Servant Savior knows nothing about self-serve lines, nor does he want us to hang around them."**

Jesus tells his followers a story about a rich farmer who had a great crop one year. But he didn't have enough barns to store it all. To remedy the situation (and maybe to impress the farmer down the road, but we don't know that for sure) this guy tears his too-small barns down and builds bigger ones. Then, with all the extra grain stored away, he gives himself permission to take life easy—eat, drink, and have a good time.

God walks into the picture and calls the man and his plans foolish. He reminds the man he could die that night and lose it all. The story's tagline reads, "That is how it will be for anyone who stores things away for himself but is not rich in God's eyes" (Luke 12:21 NIrV).

Self-serve storerooms and barns, collections of *things*. Self-serve mind-set, selfishness. The parable teaches a faith truth about freedom from self-serving attitudes, actions, and dreams. The truth is that, unless

>>LIFE AIN'T *LEAVE IT TO BEAVER—* THAT WAS CANCELLED A LONG TIME AGO.

our purpose is making sure *we* are served, self-serve lines serve little purpose when we look at things with an eternal perspective.

There's also an unexpected faith truth in the terse conversation Kim Bauer and her friend Janet York have with Rogow, a male prostitute living on the streets. Kim and Janet have been kidnapped by the boys they joined for a fun time in the middle of the night (when Jack's bad day had just begun). They plead to Rogow for help as they manage to escape and run from their abductors, "We've been kidnapped ... [Janet's] arm is broken. Those guys are still out there."

Rogow's well of compassion has dried up, and he responds matter-of-factly, "Welcome to the neighborhood."

Welcome to the neighborhood on the corner of Selfishness and Watch-Out-For-#1 streets. Rogow has enough problems—real problems—of his own. Life ain't *Leave It to Beaver*—that was cancelled a long time ago.

> **""God doesn't care if we have things; he just doesn't want our things to have us."**
>
> **—Unknown**

Our real problems may not mimic those of Kim and Janet, but since they're just as serious, maybe we've each cried out something like, "I've been kidnapped by the needs of my job and my kids. My heart is broken. Those creditor guys are still out there."

And the self-centered world yells back: "Welcome to the neighborhood! See those bootstraps—pull yourself up with 'em."

Tough neighborhoods of self-serving thoughts and greed surround us, snatching us from the aisles of life. Satan finds greed and self-absorption irresistible, so he fills our bags with them, like Bridget filled Mandy's, offering deals that seem too good to pass up.

He encourages narcissism—says, "Eat, drink, and have a good time. Focus on yourself."

"There's a line—sometimes a fine one—between greedy selfishness and healthy ambition."

Having learned the truth that Satan strives to turn my focus onto myself, I also know that things aren't as black-and-white as I've implied. There's a line—sometimes a fine one—between greedy selfishness and healthy ambition. We traipse along boldly on the side of ambition and then oops ... we trip over the line, falling headfirst onto the other side, that greed side.

God loves to gift people with a healthy—spiritually, physically, and emotionally—passion for all of life. The life motto of C. T. Studd (1860–1931), an English missionary to the people of China, India, and Africa, was "Some want to live within the sound of church or chapel bell; I want to run a rescue shop within a yard of hell."[1] That's an amazing, healthy ambition and passion for something—others' salvation. Maybe we should be known as human *do*ings rather than as human *be*ings! In our *doings*, instead of checking out, we need to create checkpoints. I've asked myself point-blank: Am I doing things, living life, just for myself, or does what I do benefit others and give God glory? Is what I'm doing giving the Devil a foothold (see Eph. 4:27) with which he can send me tumbling into the pit of self-service and greed? Am I aligned with God's will, or will God say my alignment needs service?

And as long as we're examining ourselves, it's also tempting to take a good punch in the jaw and accuse ourselves of out-of-whack priorities. We need to get ourselves off the top shelf and put Christ there, put Christ first on our priority list. On second thought ... I'm not going to do just that, because, first of all, we shouldn't put Christ on *top* of our priority list. (Wait! Before you call the heresy police, hear me out—or read me out, in this case.) Christ should hold top position in every aspect of our lives. In other words, the priority list doesn't just put Christ as number one and continue down the line with faith, family, job, etc. Rather, Christ obviously is first in our faith; he's also first in our family; first in our job, etc. If that's the case, we'll walk humbly whatever we do, giving the glory and honor in our lives to Christ instead of self. He's part of everything we do, think, and say. He's the priority in every part of our lives.

In medieval times artists didn't sign their work—didn't even consider it. (Michelangelo did sign his sculpture *Pietà* because some had attributed the work to another artist. I read he later regretted his conceit.) The artists realized their creations were gifts from God meant to draw attention away from themselves and toward the creative God of the Universe who fashioned the talent within them.

Do you remember previously I wrote that I needed a life? That life I need has been *gifted* to me—and you—in the life of Jesus Christ. I know, you're concerned about that old sin nature—so am I. Sure, our connection with Adam's sinfulness, as the Bible refers to it (see 1 Cor. 15:21–22),

> **"Welcome to God's neighborhood at the corner of Life and Forgiveness streets."**

loves making regular appearances, because it's self-absorbed and filled with greed. It wants to win us over. It wants the credit. It wants to boast about it. It wants. It wants. It wants. But we *need* to remember that sinful nature has no power. Christ checked it out and chucked it out—into a bag of garbage where it lies powerless. He went the extra step and paid for it at a special exchange rate. He took our sin and exchanged it for a forgiven life of grace. So, while that sinful nature emerges from the garbage heap of its home, it's powerless. Satan, the world, and our own sinful self can only tempt. They can't force us to do anything.

That sinful nature was the natural one in the street life Kim and Janet encountered, and it left them as it leaves us—helpless. The natural temptation for greed was too much for Mandy and Bridget. When they took Ira Gaines to the desert to retrieve the ID that would set them up for life, they instead paid the ultimate price for their greed—their own lives. (It's a good thing the *24* girls' lives are fictional, not the real thing.)

Jesus Christ has purchased a *real* life for us. The gift is free! Put away your money and coupons—they're not worth anything here. Zilch. Nada. Nothing. It's pure gift. Do you think you can handle that truth?

Welcome to God's neighborhood at the corner of Life and Forgiveness streets. No, there aren't any self-serve lines at *this* neighborhood grocery store, but the service is out of this world.

As a Matter of Fact, It's a Matter of Faith

The fundamental fact of existence is
that this trust in God, this faith,
is the firm foundation under everything that makes life worth living.
It's our handle on what we can't see.
—Hebrews 11:1 (MSG)

"But what about you?"
[Jesus] asked.
"Who do you say I am?"
—*Matthew 16:15*

>>To tell you the truth, I don't know *what* to believe.
—CTU Agent Tony Almeida,
bemused by the events surrounding him

District Director George Mason and his posse storm CTU. Mason enters, composed and self-assured, enjoying the power trip he's about to launch. He takes his place on the stairs leading to Jack's office, symbolically stepping up into the position of authority. He loves looking down on other CTU personnel. Mason authoritatively announces a lockdown of the agency offices, effective immediately. His two commandments: All personnel must remain in the building, and all communications will be monitored. Take note, George Mason is now in charge.

Mason asserts his power with words. Cautiously heading down a back hallway, Jack asserts his power with a right hook to the midsection of a guard watching the door. While the guard writhes in pain, Jack darts out the door toward his SUV. A lead in the Palmer assassination is neatly tucked inside his tactical mind.

Inside the locked agency, the odor of edginess and distrust wafts across the room. It settles on Nina and Tony as they attempt to talk nonchalantly and avoid out-and-out confrontation. Nina's displeasure with Tony is obvious in her tone and on her face. He's decided to play a childish game of tattletale—told the district office Jack's out of control and an intervention is needed.

Like a defense attorney summarizing his case, Tony calmly and quietly, so as not to draw outside attention to their dialogue, lays it out for Nina, a one-person jury.

Point one: Two CTU agents now make the LA morgue their home. And take note, ye jury of one, Jack Bauer was present when both died. Frankly, since Jack's involvement in this disaster, agents have lost faith in each other, look at each other suspiciously.

Unexpectedly, Tony takes off his all-business, lawyerlike mask and vulnerably admits to Nina what others likely feel, "To tell you the truth, I don't know what to believe."

Tony's got faith issues. Maybe we've all got faith issues. Why do we believe? Who do we believe? What is *my* belief? Does it have to be so complicated?

Is a dramatic faith testimony in order right about now? I guess that would be my cue. Where do I begin? Hmmmm.

Wait a minute, just last night I exercised amazing faith. It was the bottom of the fourth. The Cardinals were ahead. I was confident … and hungry. I

> **"I've never traveled the Damascus road— never even looked up the directions on MapQuest."**

decided to buy a hot dog from a vendor roaming the aisles. With great faith, I sent a twenty-dollar bill down the aisle as eighteen hands passed it to the vendor. Almost miraculously, not only did I receive the change back, but also the hot dog—even though the same eighteen hands had now handled my food! Talk about faith.

Let me guess—that's not the faith testimony you were looking for. Stepping into the confessional booth, I admit I'm uncomfortable when people ask me to share my testimony. Those who ask usually have their own road-to-Damascus epiclike conversion stories. By absolutely no means am I saying *anything* negative about those Spirit-created miracles of faith formations. It's just that my testimony seems so mundane in comparison. I've never traveled the Damascus road—never even looked up the directions on MapQuest. That's not to say my faith walk hasn't taken me to the proverbial mountaintop. Yes, I've also wallowed in the mud, sloshing my way through the valley of the shadow of near spiritual death—and believe me, I had no fear because *I* was with *me*. But for the most part my testimony file remains quietly categorized under *A* for average.

Ready? Hold on to your hat. I was born into a deeply committed Christian family. Baptism in the name of the Father, Son, and Holy Spirit followed about two weeks later. Since birth, I've worshipped regularly. Sunday school was part of the routine. I attended Christian elementary school, Christian high school, and Christian junior college—all requiring religion courses and regular chapel services. Marriage to a Christian young lady followed graduation from a state university. Together we worshipped at a church whose pastor inspired me to go into the seminary. Following those four years came eleven years of pastoral ministry. My wife and I have been blessed with three children in whom the Spirit has created faith. In May 2000 I stepped out in faith to begin a ministry of full-time writing and speaking. There you go. That's my faith testimony. Thaaat's all folks. Pretty exciting, wouldn't you say? I bet you were on the edge of your seats reading that dramatic account.

> **❝A faith that hasn't been tested can't be trusted.❞**
> —Adrian Rogers

Adrian Rogers' words come to mind (accompanied by some guilt, I admit). He says, "A faith that hasn't been tested can't be trusted."[1] How much has my faith been tested? If not as much as others' faith, does that mean my faith can't be trusted? Then I recall another pastor reflecting on his ministry, saying, "How come everywhere St. Paul went there was a riot, and everywhere I go there's a tea party?" Riots? No, I don't remember any of those, and you'd think something like that would stick out in my mind. Now tea parties, that's a different animal. Been there. Done those. Quaint surroundings. Mouthwatering desserts. Nonconfrontational or controversial conversations. Comfy seats in the Victorian parlors of life. Those aren't the backdrops for riots.

On the other hand (the one not holding the cup of tea), I read Martin Marty's comments in his book *Places Along the* Way regarding the faith of Abraham (who was asked to sacrifice his son Isaac), and I pump my fists in the air, cheering, "Go, Martin! Go, Martin!" Check this out: "We do not have to hear voices or seek tests of faith beyond those that come in the ordinary course of daily temptations and adventures. Even on the smaller scales of our own lives, we find the calls of God dramatic, the promises fulfilled."[2]

>> GROWING UP WITHOUT MY DAD, I FOUND A DEEP, IMPORTANT RELATIONSHIP WITH MY HEAVENLY FATHER.

I like that. Obviously I would, after describing my faith testimony as a pretty straight walk from tea party to tea party. At the same time it challenges me to explore God's work in my life and faith—to look at it from God's perspective, instead of from my tunnel-like vision.

Let me take another look.

I grew up without a father. He died in an accident at work when my mom was in the fifth month of her pregnancy. Even then, without my knowing it, God placed me in his own intensive neonatal care. Shielding me from the tragedy, he faithfully knit me together in my mother's womb, just as David tells me in Psalm 139:13–14.

Growing up without my dad, I found a deep, important relationship with my heavenly Father. While others might brag on the strengths of their own fathers, no one could come close to the work of my Father—who art in heaven.

While I grew up in the church (technically I grew up in St. Louis, but you know what I mean), God used pastors, Sunday school teachers, and faith mentors to mold my faith in what heaven would call a dramatic way, while the human view might deem it ordinary. Sometimes he even taught me through boring sermons and services that lacked the joy read about from the big Bible on the pulpit.

As a child, I'd often sit in church—with my little suit and tie but never tennis shoes—and think, "There's got to be more." The crucifix behind the altar scowled at me, the preacher yelled at me, and the congregation sounded, at least to my young ears, like monotone thespians who should be thankful God didn't write a review in the morning paper. When I thought about those things from my seat behind a pillar that blocked my view of the altar and pulpit, I wondered how and if God could use me to bring some life—God's joyful, awesome, abundant life—into the picture.

> **The congregation sounded, at least to my young ears, like monotone thespians who should be thankful God didn't write a review in the morning paper.**

Little did I know that one day God would use those experiences to nudge me into the pastoral ministry.

Like one of the notes my friend passed in church despite my mother's critical eye, the Holy Spirit passed the joy of the Lord, and it landed in my lap ... and heart. I would later serve as one of thirty-two pastors and foreign missionaries—beginning with my great-grandfather—in my family tree. What a legacy God created for me as I consider the faith of these other family members. Once again, dramatic behind-the-scenes creativity from the one who so simply (?) created the world with a few words.

At first, I didn't get that vision. After attending all smaller-sized Christian schools, I ended up at a larger public university to receive my undergraduate degree, intending to work in radio or TV. How could I know that my broadcasting experience and degree would benefit me later as I interviewed with media outlets? How could I know that God's taking me out of that sheltered community would help me better relate and minister to his people's human, and not at all sheltered, struggles? And how would I know the power of his grace would keep me safe through those college days when I ignored him?

That grace was there again as my mom died from cancer when I was twenty-five. Watching her die would fill me with Christlike compassion for others dying and for families who grieve. God would work through Mom's last words, dramatically touching—more than that—radically shaping and strengthening my faith. After an hour of lying before death's door in a comatose state, she sat up in bed, looked at her children, and to each one clearly said, "I love you, and I'll see you again." She then lay down, slipped back into the coma, and was gently and graciously carried into heaven and the arms of Jesus about an hour later. I now know that my mom, though not perfect, served as an earthly champion and heroine of my faith.

> **"After an hour of lying before death's door in a comatose state, she sat up in bed, looked at her children, and to each one clearly said, 'I love you, and I'll see you again.'"**

What about the periods of depression and anxiety attacks that later snuck into my life? While my world was darkened, I saw a cracked window that continually let in little rays of God's love, promises, and presence. I even see now that my struggles with depression and subsequent sharing about them actually encourage others.

My faith explodes as I see the Spirit clearly and miraculously create growth spurts in the faith of our children.

I see and shout, "Thank you, Father, for working through so many situations and people to strengthen, encourage, and restore my faith." You gave me friends, coworkers, laughter, illness, funerals, books, music, conversations, worship services, prayer time, entertaining times, quiet times, goofy times, and even—maybe *especially*—ordinary times.

Now that I think of it, I could fill volumes with a faith testimony. And mundane wouldn't describe it. The volumes would spill over with heavenly-directed drama and miraculous conversions from ...

- baptism to forgiveness and the new beginning it offers;
- depression to smiles, laughter, and even more laughter;
- mentors in the faith to a great cloud of witnesses to God's grace;
- God's creation of good from bad, to his power made perfect in my weakness;
- my first attempt at singing "Jesus Loves the Little Children" (from a faith-filled heart) to the Spirit-created faith that allows me to boldly confess, "Jesus, you are the Christ, the Son of the Living God. You are my Lord and Savior. I love you, but more miraculously, you love me."

So, who do *you* say that he is?

There's Stability in an Unstable Environment

Keep your eyes on *Jesus*, who both began and finished this race we're in. Study how he did it. Because he never lost sight of where he was headed.... When you find yourselves flagging in your faith, go over that story again, item by item, that long litany of hostility he plowed through. *That* will shoot adrenaline into your souls!

—Hebrews 12:2–3 (MSG)

sta·ble (stā′bəl) adj.: *Consistently dependable; steadfast of purpose.*

—The American Heritage Dictionary of the English Language, Fourth Edition

>>You don't trust me, but you trust Jack? Come on, Nina, he's been lying; he's been hiding things from us. It might be okay for you, but it's not okay for me.

—Tony Almeida to Nina Myers

Is Jack stable?
He's on the run like a fugitive.
Is Jack stable?
He bucks protocol.
Is Jack stable?
He's guilty of insubordination.
Is Jack stable?
He works through unknown channels.
Is Jack stable?
He's turned CTU into an unstable environment.
Is Jack stable?

>>You don't trust me, but you trust Jack?

>> MY FRIEND DESCRIBED [*24's*]
AVERAGE VIEWERS AS INDEPENDENT
THINKERS AND ADRENALINE JUNKIES.

A faster-paced, more intense television show than *24* would be difficult to name. My friend described its average viewers as independent thinkers and adrenaline junkies. Adrenaline junkies. I really like that description. I also like the fact that God knows whether we fit that description or not, and whether we admit it or not, we either do now or will at some time in the future long for security.

I'm picturing you now, Mr. or Ms. Adrenaline Junkie. Hmmm ... not exactly a picture of someone craving stability. You're on the move because, even though you have it all, you want more. You love the extreme. You live on the edge and are comfortable there. But you independent thinkers can easily hide the fact that you need a stable environment, even as you confidently maneuver your way into life's six-lane rush-hour traffic.

> "Jesus knew about long days and sometimes-longer nights."

The psalmists are great examples of God's adrenaline-loving but maybe not-so-self-confident people. They put up with so much, struggle so openly with their faith. David, in Psalm 13, describes one of his adrenaline-producing moments. I hope you'll take time to read it.

What is it that gets the adrenaline flowing for the psalmist? Physical challenges? Danger around? Life challenges? I've been there. I imagine you have too. Long days, restless nights, discomfort of one kind or another, discontent. Maybe some things we independent thinkers can't, or shouldn't, tackle on our own.

In those times we, like David the psalmist, find that God is faithful to his promises, and we can throw ourselves headlong into his strong and saving arms.

> "The Roman adrenaline junkies at the cross mocked the stability the man being crucified promised God's people."

Jesus knew about long days and sometimes-longer nights. The twenty-four hours that led up to his death constituted, arguably, the longest day of his life. Roman nails and a Father's love pinned him to a cross-shaped tree where his weakened and bloodied body looked its frailest.

What I've never been able

>>STABILITY IS A DESIRE OF THE SOUL.

to understand is that Roman soldiers saw crucifixion as a sport—one we might today label a sick, extreme sport. Picture them. Watching the criminal writhe. Spitting at the soon-to-be corpse. Gambling for personal belongings that the dead won't be taking with him. Getting a charge out of blood streaming from the flesh around the nail holes—the more blood, the more they cheered. The Roman adrenaline junkies at the cross mocked the stability the man being crucified promised God's people. Stability? Who needs it? They were in control, secure in themselves, and living on the adrenaline of the moment. "Save yourself! Come down from the cross, if you are the Son of God!" challenged the jeering crowd (Matt. 27:40).

People with this modus operandi hide their great insecurities under a mask of self-confidence. Stability is a desire of the soul, however. We'd be wise to admit that to ourselves, to God, and even to others. Walking around with our hearts exposed and the needs and wounds of our souls in plain view leaves us vulnerable, I know. But hey, those wounds will heal if they're cleaned with forgiveness and grace and then left uncovered to air.

Worship leader Nathan Lawrence's song "Sweet Lamb of God" takes me to Christ's cross, where I find healing for *my* exposed wounds, and hints at what my response to that healing might be. Care to join me there, friends?

> A thorny crown on a kingly head, How could it be?
> Three nails between Your joints; Those nails were
>   meant for me.
> Your pained yet loving eyes
> Survey the crowds below
> Their hearts full of hatred

A sea of sinful souls
That one there—that one is me!
I taunt and jeer
But with arms stretched open wide You are
    welcoming me near

Oh, oh sweet Lamb of God
You take away my sin
And let me in Your presence again
Alleluia to the Lamb[1]

You're right, Nathan. We've walked among those Romans at the foot of the cross. We've used our adrenaline to make a mockery of Jesus' salvation, ignoring what he's done and expecting to be in control of our own situations. The Romans' problem wasn't too much adrenaline. It was adrenaline wrongly focused. Is that our problem too?

> **"The Romans' problem wasn't too much adrenaline. It was adrenaline wrongly focused. Is that our problem too?"**

I need (yes, *need*) to share the annual Christmas letter my friends received from a ministry family who lives in a vulnerable area of the inner city that cries out for stability and grace. Talk about adrenaline correctly focused. (*Names have been changed.*)

We want to tell you about T.J. who is being raised by his mother, who suffers from schizophrenia. T.J. is a quiet, even-tempered teenager who is trying to finish school, yet has to deal with a drug-addicted brother who beats up him and his mother every month or so. His girlfriend will be giving birth to their child in a few months. Surely, T.J. is one of the faces at the manger this year.

We are also traveling with Kendall who told his peers he was a homosexual more than a year ago, but is trying to come to terms with what it all means now. His dad is quite ill and his mother has had a nervous breakdown. The school gave Kendall clothes, but he is ashamed of his whole person, his whole life, so he seldom comes to school. On Saturday, my husband will take Kendall for a haircut and conversation. They will talk about Kendall being robbed at gunpoint, and how he was made to strip, and how none of this is his fault. Surely, Kendall is anxious for the Christ Child this year.

Lorna spent the night here last night. She had no change of clothes because her mother has sold them all to support her drug addiction. Lorna lives in a crack house—her mother's house—with her younger brother and sisters, and whoever else is passing through. Lorna is an extremely quiet girl who watches everything. There are strange, older men hanging out at her house these days. Talking to her. Telling her how pretty she is. Touching her. We are hurrying to get Lorna to the manger.

Tony is like a son to us. He is with us weekly, often for days at a time. He is one of the lead voices in the Youth Choir and a gifted visual artist. He spends most of his time thinking. Just thinking. Earlier this year, Tony started selling drugs because he and his brothers had nothing to eat when they awakened each morning. He is presently in the ninth grade for a second time and still has less than a 1.0 grade point average on a 4.0 scale. Tony wants to be an architect. Our deal with Tony is this: Each time he pulls a grade up, we will enroll him in an art class at a local Art and Design Institute. He starts a drawing class in January and an improvisational composition class in February. Tony arrived at the stable, in advance, found some wood, and built the manger.

There are so many traveling to Bethlehem who will be at the manger with us. Hoping. Waiting. Expecting this baby to make things okay in this world. This divine baby also wants to use our hands. Our voices. Our compassion.

I hope you are not traveling to the manger alone this year. I hope there are young people, frail people, poor people, and even strong people journeying with you.

>> **THERE'S NOTHING WRONG WITH RUNNING ON ADRENALINE *IF* THE ADRENALINE COMES DIRECTLY FROM THE STABLE HEART OF THE SAVIOR AND PUMPS FEROCIOUSLY AND FREELY THROUGH THE HOLY VEINS OF THE SOUL.**

This couple recognized there's security in a stable environment, the stable environment of Jesus' love, the stable environment that's found sometimes in the most unusual, out-of-the-way places:

- a Bethlehem stable that is home to a newborn baby
- a surgery waiting room filled with hope, peace, and yes, even moments of contentment
- a father unknowingly teaching his child a life-changing faith truth, by his own example
- a mother disclosing a teachable moment to her child as they drive to school
- a hug, without words spoken, at a funeral home
- an employer's encouraging words and prayers for employees

- a bar where an alcoholic exchanges a beer for a prayer
- a makeshift chapel in the middle of a war zone
- outside an empty Jerusalem garden tomb where our fears of death were miraculously stabilized by new life

For Jack Bauer and all of us who lead adrenaline-driven, sometimes not-so-stable lives, there's nothing wrong with running on adrenaline *if* the adrenaline comes directly from the stable heart of the Savior and pumps ferociously and freely through the holy veins of the soul. He is our stabilizer (1 Cor. 1:8–9).

Deception Can Be Deceiving

Senator Palmer asks, "How do we justify the cover-up?"
His chief of staff responds, "The voters know how to forgive. You just have to know how to ask for it."

God guards knowledge with a passion, but he'll have nothing to do with deception.

—Proverbs 22:12 (MSG)

>>(Silence)

—From the car Alan York drives, Teri Bauer sitting in the passenger's seat, completely unaware that Alan's playing a game of deception—
he's not who he says he is

>>How does Jack keep his composure? He must
have been hangin' with Tony Soprano! That's a
dead body in the trunk! And he doesn't have a
clue whose it is!

Don't worry about Jack. Lifeless bodies don't faze him. He's seen his share of 'em! In fact, he's killed his share! And if he needs an ID, CTU can handle that in no time flat.

>>How does Jack keep his composure? He's got
his Clint Eastwood game face on, even though
when Gaines calls him he's in the middle of
the hospital corridor, with Teri and Alan York
next to him!

What do you mean? Jack has to go along with Gaines—he has no choice. He has to play the game even if it's a game of blackmail ... even if his family is the bargaining chip. Man, he's doing it for his family!

>>How does Jack keep his composure? Does he
have Norman Bates's blood running through
him? Gaines plays him like a puppet. "Walk
down this hall; walk down that hall. Go to the
parking garage. Get in that car. Get the
earpiece out of the glove compartment. Put it
in your ear. You're taking orders from me. I
can see your every move." Come on, man,
Jack's a hero, and heroes aren't puppets!

Sure, he appears to have lost control, but you know Jack will cut the puppet strings. "If you hurt my daughter I will kill you," he says menacingly before he throws his cell phone out the window at Gaines' command.

>>Okay, but how does Teri keep any composure? She's been duped into thinking Alan York sits next to her, driving the car. So when she finds out during a phone call from Nina that the body in the trunk has been ID'd as Alan York, she knows she's sharing a ride with one of Gaines' thugs. How the heck does she keep any composure?

You got me there. I'd lose it, lunch and all.

I admit it. I'm no Jack Bauer. Oh, you're not surprised? Put me in Jack or Teri's position, and I'll have no composure; in fact, I'll probably start *decomposing* on the spot.

Here's an example of this fact, and how, unlike Jack, I was stupidly (and humorously) duped. First, though, let me defend my actions a little. This took place over twenty years

> **"From the time we landed until we got to the hotel, I checked my Captain Marvel secret hideaway, bulletproof wallet 327 times."**

ago—I'd just graduated from college and gotten married. I was young, okay! (FYI—though it contains some obvious hyperbole, the following story is true.)

It all started when I opened an invitation to a family wedding in New York City. As I read it, the ol' stomach butterflies woke up and fluttered like crazy. New York City. THE City. The Big Apple. The city that doesn't sleep.

I had never been to "The City." Apples aren't my favorite fruit. And I need my sleep.

From the news reports, movies, Mets and Yankees games on TV, and my vivid imagination, I had drawn a mental picture of what "The City" was all about. As I prepared for the trip, I took time to visualize every possible way I could get mugged. Then I checked prices for mace, money belts, and bodyguards.

> **❝We'd allowed deception to unnecessarily sneak into our minds without an invitation.❞**

From the time we landed until we got to the hotel, I checked my Captain Marvel secret hideaway, bulletproof wallet 327 times. It was unharmed, still strapped to my chest.

Walking down the street with my family the day of the wedding, I observed everything that moved. My wary eyes darted from one side of the street to the other and then to the rooftops, searching for snipers possibly hidden there.

Wait a minute! Quiet everyone. What was that knocking sound? We all stopped in our tracks. There it was again, coming from inside the trunk of the car parked next to me! I could not believe it! (This really is true, folks!) As the knocking continued, I pictured the poor soul inside, badly beaten, bound and gagged. We couldn't just ignore his cries and walk on by. I stepped away and froze, plastering myself against a brick wall. (Remember, I'm no Jack Bauer.) My father-in-law moved to the car and cautiously knocked on the trunk. "Are you okay? (Pause) Can you hear me?" No response. He knocked again. Then one more time. "Are you okay?" he said louder, trying not to create a New York City theatrical scene.

Then it happened. My father-in-law positioned his head so his ear lay directly on the trunk of the car. We held our breath ... until we burst out laughing! Out from under the car rolled a man with a hammer. He'd been working on his muffler!

We'd allowed deception to unnecessarily sneak into our minds without an invitation.

The rest of the trip was great. I even traded my New York–proof wallet for an "I *heart* NY" bumper sticker.

That was not the first time deception got the best of me (although it's the funniest). I've even deceived myself, justifying my sins—whitewashing them with diluted paint. In certain situations I've talked a good game while my heart and soul really weren't into it. At times, I've easily related to Eugene Peterson's translation of James 1:26 in *The Message*: "Anyone who sets himself up as 'religious' by talking a good game is self-deceived. This kind of religion is hot air and only hot air."

> **❝I've even deceived myself, justifying my sins—whitewashing them with diluted paint.❞**

>> SOME DECEPTIONS MAY *SEEM* INSIGNIFICANT, BUT THAT'S BECAUSE DECEPTIONS CAN BE DECEIVING.

I imagine you join me in having experienced people who deliberately deceive. They lie. They laugh behind our backs at our gullibility. They love to see us fall—sometimes quite hard. Yet when they get caught in their deceptive acts, they laugh it off and walk away without realizing they're playing with fire. Eugene Peterson paraphrases the wise one who writes, "People who shrug off deliberate deceptions, saying, 'I didn't mean it, I was only joking,' are worse than careless campers who walk away from smoldering campfires" (Prov. 26:18–19 MSG).

Some deceptions may *seem* insignificant, but that's because deceptions can be deceiving. If we do the deceiving, we probably don't realize the ramifications for the deceived. A crisis of faith. A bruised reputation. A shattered self-concept. A torn relationship. And don't think this only happens in the community of unbelievers. If you believe that, you're being deceived by the greatest of deceivers, Satan.

> **❝Satan offers quite an assortment of lies to hang our hats on.❞**

I've learned over the years that when dealing with a deceiver, Scripture would have us deal with him or her quickly, honestly, and directly, with love and forgiveness our motives. Some of us hate confrontation; others thrive on it. Wherever you stand on the subject, hang on to that Christian love motive, hoping to win the other person over—not with deception, but with an honest desire that sin be confessed and forgiveness received. The obvious next step isn't easy to take—release that person from guilt over the deception; give that person into the hands of the One who is not capable of deception, but loves to see the reception of forgiveness by his people.

The great deceiver, Satan, offers quite an assortment of lies to hang our hats on. "When he lies, he speaks his native language, for he is a liar and the father of lies" (John 8:44). Can you relate to any of the following falsities from the great deceiver?

- I'm a good person; so are the majority of people.
- Everyone *must* like and approve of me.
- I have to do good to earn God's favor.
- God won't use me unless my faith is strong.
- While some talk about something called "Christ-esteem," I know it's all about high *self*-esteem.

Satan even tries to convince us there's no hope for our sorry condition. Is there hope? The Paul of the New Testament, then known as Saul, for a time thrived on persecuting Christians as Satan's deception permeated his being. He would have single-handedly wiped out the whole Christian community. But that all happened before he met Jesus Christ. The Master had other plans for Saul (see Acts 9:1–31). Changing his name from Saul to Paul, God's Spirit inspired him to become undoubtedly the greatest evangelist the world has ever seen. He went from being deceived to being dedicated to declaring freedom from Satan's power in Christ. Truth reigned in his life from that day on. In fact, he wrote,

> Since God has so generously let us in on what he is doing, we're not about to throw up our hands and walk off the job just because we run into occasional hard times. We refuse to wear masks and play games. We don't maneuver and manipulate behind the scenes. And we don't twist God's Word to suit ourselves. Rather, we keep everything we do and say out in the open, the whole truth on display, so that those who want to can see and judge for themselves in the presence of God. (2 Cor. 4:1–2 MSG)

So the next time we're in circumstances like Teri Bauer's, knowing we're being deceived and yet powerless to combat the deceiver, let's compose ourselves and realize there's hope. There's forgiveness. In Christ, there's power to say "No!" Through faith in Jesus, God offers transformation for our deceiving and deceived lives.

When Satan, the consummate lying deceiver, comes nudging his way into our minds, we'll just lie back ... into the protective, compassionate, and strong arms of our Savior, Jesus Christ. We're never too old to be held.

FAITH TRUTH #7
Unexpected Freedom Comes to Unsuspecting Prisoners

The Spirit of the Sovereign
LORD is on me....
He has sent me to bind up the
brokenhearted,
to proclaim freedom for the
captives
and release from darkness for
the prisoners ...
to bestow on them a crown of
beauty instead of ashes,
the oil of gladness instead of
mourning,
and a garment of praise
instead of a spirit of despair.
—Isaiah 61:1, 3

*We overestimate
our power and
underestimate God's.*

—Don Clair

>>*Rick, help me get out of
here!*
>>How? This place is like a
prison.
>>*People break out of prison
all the time.*
—Conversation between Kim
and Rick

>>Rick, help me get out of here!

I'm a dead woman walking. They're out there. Can't you hear them plotting against me—against you, too, Rick? What's that? Sounds like they're loading their weapons. I'm not paranoid, just rightfully afraid. We've got to get out of here. I need an escape plan. And I need your help.

>>Rick, help me get out of here!

Lose the flimsy excuses. Forget the boundary fence. Do you really think prison fences keep prisoners from executing escapes? Get real, Rick. And while you're at it get rid of your naive delusions—Gaines has no purpose for you. Don't fool yourself; you're a dead man walking too.

>>Rick, help me get out of here!

I'm guessing similar pleas for help have surfaced in your mind lately? Let's get real, friends.

>>HELP ME GET OUT OF THIS RUT THAT BORES ME TO TEARS.

Help me get out of this dead-end job that's driving me nuts.
Help me get out of this habit that's strangling me and my faith.
Help me get out of this loveless marriage.
Help me get out of this body that stares back at me in the mirror.
Help me get out of this debt that's burying me alive.
Help me get out of this rut that bores me to tears.
Help me get out of this addiction that has taken over my mind and life.
Help me get out of here.

How? It's like a prison.
People get out of prison all the time, right?
An escape plan must be devised.

> **"I flunked Common Sense 101 but still graduated with honors from life's How Dense Can I Be? doctorate program."**

I'll never forget my time in prison. I had the privilege to share hope through Christ with a death row inmate while supporting his desire to allow God to change him.

Okay, that's not the only time I've spent in prison. My choice to sin locks me up again and again. I don't understand why I keep returning to sin's prison when Christ has set me free. It's like I flunked Common Sense 101 but still graduated with honors from life's How Dense Can I Be? doctorate program.

I can relate to Otis on the old *Andy Griffith Show.* Otis walks around free as a bird until he encounters his old friends Mr. Beam and Mr. Daniels. Soon Otis realizes what he's done—again—and staggers into the sheriff's office. He stumbles into the prison cell, slams the barred door behind him, and lies down in the sludge of his habitual sin.

Otis, my man, I can relate—not to the drinking, but to your course of action. No doubt about it—God's children are free in Christ. We can bask in that freedom. But just as we get comfortable, familiar friends—Mr. Bitterness, Miss Self-only, and Mr. and Mrs. Lusty—invite us to hang out. Let the party begin! And let guilt bring an end to the big bash. We meet up with Otis at the prison doors and try to get comfortable within our little cells, making our own beds to lie in.

> **"We struggle to survive our own reality show!"**

The mornings after Otis's self-imposed lockdowns, he reaches through the bars, grabs the key on the wall, and lets himself out. Otis can leave on his own—we can't. We struggle to survive our own reality show!

Spending Otis-time in the prison of my sins, I've learned that incarceration by sin and its life-prison compares to the reality of penitentiary life. The death row prisoner I referred to previously confirmed that when he wrote these words from his prison cell:

> There are too many problems here to list: revenge, jealousy, deceit, and false information are daily occurrences here. It is extremely difficult to deal with the day to day environment here in prison, not to mention all the scheming that goes with it. I am not proud of where I am, or what I did to get here. I was forced to come to grips with reality a long time ago.

Sound familiar? Read that passage again. As you come to the word *prison*, insert the location of the spiritual, emotional, or physical prison in which you're living (e.g., my workplace, my home, my relationships, my school). Life in a penitentiary can easily mirror our lives outside the prison walls. Scary, isn't it? Like Rick in *24*, we may need a reality check regarding our chances of survival—will we remain confined, or is freedom our calling?

The reality is that we need a rescuer—a Savior—and one stands ready to set us free. Our key to freedom hangs at his side—his side once pierced by a Roman spear. He holds that key in his hand—his nail-scarred hand. Stepping gingerly out of our cells into freedom, we find the Savior has provided fresh, clean clothes, made of wrinkle-free forgiveness and laundered in the stain-removing detergent of his own blood. It's obvious his freedom comes with a complete and eternal love.

Can our independent nature accept this love? Or do we hesitate at the door, wondering *why* he would love us? We're not the only prisoners contemplating these questions. After prison missionary Don Clair shared a message of hope through Christ's love to a hundred inmates, an elderly man sat crying. After forty-one years behind bars, the man was scheduled for release the following week. The tearful man told Don, "It never, ever even remotely crossed my mind that God could love someone like me."

The man was imprisoned behind bars *and* behind his sin and guilt for decades. He figured he never had a chance at knowing the love of God. Why is Christ's grace so hard to accept? to believe? to live with? Maybe our independent spirits, our need for control, our invincible egos, or our fears someone will discover we actually need love and acceptance restrain us. We're so used to living with guilt that we forget what it's like to live without it. We wonder why God would give us the time of day, especially when we have a plethora of electronic gizmos to do that. But it's not uncommon to struggle with the truth that God loves us.

> **"It never, ever even remotely crossed my mind that God could love someone like me."**

Why not confess our selfish pride and all the barnacles of sin attached, asking the Lord to forgive us and to free us from the prisons we've become comfortable in? These days we're not used to—let alone comfortable with—confessing that we're in the wrong. Someone's tattooed "What's the big deal?" and "It's not hurting anyone" on our minds. But that goes against God's carefully devised plan for our escape from life's prison of sin, guilt, and hopelessness.

His plan suggests we do the following:

- Admit our need for a Savior. Ask for a release from the prison of our sin.

- Don't overestimate our power or underestimate God's. He even works in the most out-of-the-way places and in the most stubborn hearts.

- Rejoice as Christ lovingly unlocks prison cells with his key to life. Removing our heavy chains of guilt, he says, "I forgive," promising to remember the sin no more—not hold it against us in any way; empowering us to forgive ourselves and others. Acting on that forgiveness is rarely a cakewalk, by the way, so Christ baked the proverbial file into the cake allowing us to cut through the cell bars that separate us from others, restoring our relationships with them through his example of forgiveness—not saying their actions (or ours) are okay, but celebrating the freedom from sin's bitterness and pain.

- Realize Christ already signed our release papers. When the door opens, we'll step out of the dark into the light of peace and grace.

Paul and Silas (Acts 16:16–34) lived thankful, peace-filled lives— even while confined in a real prison because others didn't like God working through them. While chained in a dungeon, they find peace in praying and singing hymns—loudly enough that the other prisoners could hear.

> **❝A heart at peace gives life to the body.❞**
> —Proverbs 14:30

Around midnight, a violent earthquake causes their cell doors to open and their chains to break loose. Freedom calls their names, yet both they and their fellow prisoners stay put. The warden, realizing this can only happen by the power of the living God, asks Paul and Silas, "What must I do to be saved?" The men respond, "Believe in the Lord Jesus, and you will be saved—you and your household" (vv. 30–31).

>>A KEY TO FREEDOM HANGS ON A NAIL FROM THE CROSS ON WHICH JESUS DIED.

The apostles share the freeing gospel of Jesus Christ with the warden and prisoners. Later, they baptize that warden and his family, whose lives God transforms by the powerful Word and ways of Christ working through two prisoners who live in the freedom and joy of knowing Christ's love and forgiveness.

The miraculous, freeing gift of peace is available by grace, through faith in Jesus Christ. A key to freedom hangs on a nail from the cross on which Jesus died. Another one lies on top of slightly worn burial cloths inside an empty Easter tomb.

Wait! You don't have to go to Jerusalem to get a freedom key. And you don't need someone like Rick to help you find freedom, either. No, your Savior comes to you and unlocks your cell and prison chains. Don't underestimate Christ's power, love, or forgiveness. He comes with unexpected freedom for unsuspecting prisoners. Get ready to celebrate! Get ready to *live!*

>>LORD,

>>I HAVE HAD ENOUGH. ENOUGH GUILT AND SHAME TO LAND ME IN SOLITARY CONFINEMENT. MY SECRET SINS MAY BE HIDDEN FROM OTHERS, BUT NOT FROM YOU. OPEN THE WAY OF ESCAPE FOR ME TO LIVE, NOT AS A FUGITIVE ON THE RUN, BUT AS A CHILD OF GOD RUNNING TO YOU FOR PERFECT PEACE AND FORGIVENESS.

>>Transform my mind to your truth that continually sets me free. Forgive me for (confess to the Lord specifically what has imprisoned you). Help me to avoid the evil that drags me back to the "cell of separation" from you and others.

>>Thank you, Lord, for serving my life sentence, so I may be sentenced to eternal life with you.

>>In the name of Jesus I pray. Amen.

Love Covers a Multitude of Fears

God is love. When we take up permanent residence in a life of love, we live in God and God lives in us.
—1 John 4:16 (MSG)

We are going to get through this, I promise you.

—Teri,
as she holds Kim

>>I'm trying to explain to you what a simple, powerful thing my love for you is. No matter how bad things get or how good they get, that's not going to change. I just don't know how to do anything but love you.

—Teri Bauer to daughter, Kim

A tornado of fear wreaks havoc on mother and daughter.

>>The clock is ticking ...

Teri and Kim lie waiting in the path of the storm's eye; they huddle together in the locked waiting room of the offices of Apprehension, Dread, and Associates, Ltd.

An inferno of emotional devotion bursts into flames within Teri's heart, as their terrifying hostage situation stokes the love she has for Kim.

>>The clock is ticking ...

Teri doesn't know how to do anything but love her daughter, and not just in the flaming heat of this moment ... always!

An earthquake of uncertainty rocks Kim's foundation, as she wonders if her mom's passionate words quake from a premonition of deadly tremors still to come.

> **"Above all, love each other deeply, because love covers over a multitude of sins."**
> **—1 Peter 4:8**

>>The clock is ticking ...

Are her mom's words of love signaling the end is in sight?

During my teen years I was in love with love. Maybe I haven't changed that much. Embarrassed, I share this story. My senior year in high school I told my friend, in all seriousness, that I couldn't wait to get married because then I wouldn't have to deal with all the junk we dealt with—life would be so much easier. (I'll wait until you stop laughing before I continue.) That's what you call naive, dumb, and inexperienced. My view of love was terribly distorted. Love and marriage would cover and protect me from a multitude of problems. (Oh, like you never had any outrageous views in your younger days—so you can just stop judging me, okay!?)

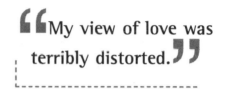

> "My view of love was terribly distorted."

Years later, *without* the assistance of a psychiatrist, I realized what *probably* lay behind this need for love. It was fear. My mom raised me alone. After my dad's fatal accident, she never remarried. I know my sister Cathy helped a lot in my formative years. I'm sure my brothers helped too, but wait a minute ... come to think about it, when Mom asked my brother Ted to watch me while I sat in one of those bouncy seats, he let me bounce right off the table! I landed headfirst on a concrete floor. But I digress.

Anyway, my mom and sister, along with my aunt and a couple of my mom's friends, filled my life with love. My life was secure until ... I can't remember how old I was when it began, but often I'd go to bed fearful. I'd visualize or dream about horrible ways Mom would die—car accidents, gunshots, explosions. You name it, I thought it.

>>FEAR AND LOVE—DIAMETRICAL OPPOSITES. BUT OPPOSITES OFTEN ATTRACT.

And her death would mean I'd be left alone, since my brothers and sisters were by then off at college or married. Don't get me wrong, I had a wonderful childhood—except for these nightmares ... and, of course, the bouncy chair incident.

Inadvertently, this fear caused me to cling to *love*—or my definition of it—in case something happened to her. I realize that now, looking back. (Incidentally, Mom's death many years later was an amazingly peaceful and Christ-centered moment—not at all like any of my nightmares.)

Fear and love—diametrical opposites. But opposites often attract. Some folks fear being loved. Others fear not finding love. There are those in love with fear and those who fear being in love. For some, perhaps especially those expecting a divorce down the road, love seems tainted by fear and uncertainty.

> **"But standing ready to conquer that fear is love."**

Love takes on a variety of modes. There's love of family and friends. Superficial love. Lust disguised as love. Unhealthy love. Guilt-induced love. One-sided love. Infatuation confused with love. The love of material objects. Love of brothers and sisters in Christ. And I'd be remiss if I passed over perfect love that casts out fear. I can't take credit for that truth. The inspired writer John penned it in 1 John 4:18. Check out the surrounding words:

> God is love. Whoever lives in love lives in God, and God in him. In this way, love is made complete among us so that we will have confidence on the day of judgment, because in this world we are like him. There is no fear in love. But perfect love drives out fear, because fear has to do with punishment. The one who fears is not made perfect in love.
> (1 John 4:16–18)

Interesting. John associates fear with punishment. I usually don't think of fear in that way; although I guess (like most people) I, too, deal with the obvious fear-punishment connection—my own mortality. Is punishment what we fear about the last day? I mean, that's what all of us deserve, right? We have it coming to us.

But standing ready to conquer that fear is love. God *is* love. His love came bundled in baby clothes. His name? Jesus. He took up the call to love and ended up taking all the punishment we deserve upon himself when he went to the cross.

It's hard to wrap our minds and faith around that truth. When our eyes are directed to the cross, we think about the physical pain Jesus endured. That's hard enough to understand. But to consider a Father—*the* Father—turning his divine back on his Son, forsaking him momentarily, so all wrath and punishment for our sins could be heaped upon Jesus. That's hard to fathom. Yet it's true.

What usually connects people's fear with punishment lies in what has been given some fearful names: Judgment Day. The Last Day. The Day of Accountability. Those names will strike fear in anyone's heart. Let's go back to what John wrote: "There is no fear in love. But perfect love drives out fear, because fear has to do with punishment" (1 John 4:18). So where's the love that covers a multitude of fears? It's

> **"The writers of the show could have taken that right out of Jesus' mouth!"**

in the fact that when Christ returns, we will *not* be judged on our lives overflowing with sin. Jesus Christ will stand between us and the Father and in essence say, "Judge this child of yours on the basis of my perfect life, not on his imperfect one." He envelops us with love, which covers a multitude of our fears and all of our sins. There is no fear in God's perfect love—an example for us in our calling to love others.

Picture Teri and Kim huddled together, trembling, in the storage barn where they expect to be killed. Teri holds Kim, hoping her love will calm her daughter's fears. Teri says, "No matter how bad things get or how good they get, [my love] is not going to change. I just don't know how to do anything but love you."

Did you catch that unexpected faith truth wrapped up in Teri's words? The writers of the show could have taken that right out of Jesus' mouth! Picture him huddling close, sharing his gift of love, calming our fears—no matter how bad things get or how good they get.

For me, that picture is similar to one from a story in the book *Blue Like Jazz* by Donald Miller. The image of the unexpected gift of love amidst fear is quite vivid.

> **"Even love for a stranger can cover a multitude of fears."**

Miller shares the story told to him of Navy SEALs performing a covert operation, freeing hostages from a building in some dark part of the world. They flew in by helicopter, made their way to the compound, and stormed the hostages' room. It was filthy and dark. The hostages were curled up in a corner, terrified. Upon the SEALs' entry, the hostages gasped in fear. The SEALs stood at the door and reassured the prisoners they were Americans. They asked the hostages to follow them out, but the hostages wouldn't. Instead, they sat on the floor and hid their eyes in fear. Their minds were stupefied, and they doubted their rescuers were really American.

The SEALs didn't know what to do; they couldn't carry all the prisoners out. One of the SEALs got an idea. He put down his weapon, took off his helmet, and curled up tightly among the hostages, getting so close his body touched some of theirs. He softened the look on his face and put his arms around them. He became one of them. The prison guards wouldn't have done this. He stayed there momentarily until some of the hostages' eyes cautiously met his. He whispered that the Americans were there to rescue them. "Will you follow us?" he asked. The hero rose to his feet, and one of the hostages did the same, then another, until all of them were willing to go. Yes, shortly thereafter, all the hostages boarded an American aircraft carrier to safety.[1]

Powerful stuff. Powerful love ... that covered a multitude of fears.

Even love for a stranger can cover a multitude of fears. One evening, while serving as a hospital on-call chaplain, I met a young girl who was rushed into the ER. A long laceration ran from her hairline to the back of her head following an automobile accident. Her mother had just been pronounced DOA. The doctors needed permission to operate, yet they couldn't locate any family. The decision to stitch the gash in her head without anesthetic was made because the doctors didn't know her health background. The doctors asked me to stand by and do what I could to calm the girl's fears and help her deal with the pain. I held her head and whispered calming words and a prayer. Maybe a calming song would help, I decided. My brain froze. The only song I could think of was "You Are My Sunshine." I must have sung it fifty times while the doctors worked and I stood fearing for the girl's motherless future and hurting with her—more for her troubled heart than her head. The next day I replayed the ordeal in my mind, and I realized what song I should have sung. It's filled with love, comfort, and good news. It's a surprisingly deep, theologically strong love song that could soothe the most fearful of hearts. Anna B. Warner wrote it in 1860:

> Jesus loves me! This I know,
> For the Bible tells me so;
> Little ones to Him belong;
> They are weak, but He is strong.

Why didn't I sing that? It's the ultimate oldie-but-goodie. Isn't *every* child comforted by those words and its familiar melody? I know *this* child is. I pray you are too.

> Yes! Jesus loves me! Yes! Jesus loves [you]!
> Yes! Jesus loves [us]! The Bible tells [us] so.

FAITH TRUTH #9
There's a Genesis for Every Problem

gen·e·sis (jĕn'Ĭ-sĭs) n.:
1. The coming into being of something; the origin. [2. the first book of the Old Testament]

—The American Heritage Dictionary of the English Language, Fourth Edition

Sighing comes to me instead of food; my groans pour out like water. What I feared has come upon me; what I dreaded has happened to me. I have no peace, no quietness; I have no rest, but only turmoil.
—Job 3:24–26

>>You're not the only one who has problems, Jack.
—Lauren, Jack's hostage

Jack Bauer's heart beats twice as fast as a ticking clock. It pounds in his chest as he runs feverishly from government agents. The handcuffs around his wrists don't appear to deter him. His mind hears the ticking clock; time is at a premium—for him and, more importantly, for his wife and daughter.

Jumping a fence, Jack rolls uncontrollably down an embankment onto a street. Despite cuffed hands, he scrambles to his feet, steadies himself, and points his cocked gun at the first oncoming vehicle. A late-model station wagon with a terrorized woman behind the wheel wins the Jack Bauer carjacking raffle. The CTU agent, suddenly turned hostage taker, jumps into her car's passenger seat. Driving directions fly out of Jack's mouth like a blast from a machine gun. The last voice-bullet takes them into a construction-site parking lot, where they invade an unmanned office trailer complete with the phone Jack covets.

Connecting with CTU, he rolls his Nina-do list off his tongue. Car. *Check.* Com unit. *Check.* Ammunition. *Check.* Locksmith kit. *Check.* Now it's Nina's turn. Dirty agent. *Check.* Jamey. *Check and underline!* As though moving in slow motion, Jack sits. A blank stare—no, a look of disbelief overcomes him. Seconds later, Jack comes out of the trance, his body transfused with anger, all directed toward Jamey, his trusted colleague turned traitor. He'd love to have a piece of her mind if his own crisis wasn't staring him in the face. End of conversation. *Click.*

Somehow, turning somewhat genial, Jack turns his attention toward the spider he has caught in his escape web and learns she has a name and a life. Her name, pinned to a uniform from an all-night diner, reads "Lauren." She's dumbfounded by the entire situation. *Who are you?* Laura quickly assumes he's a criminal who's kidnapped her, but then he begins to show her signs of a very different disposition. His words even teeter on the verge of compassion.

Bravely, Lauren speaks up, "You're not the only one who has problems, Jack. I just came off a hellacious night shift. I'm due in court in 45 minutes on a DUI charge, of which I'm guilty. So, you know, good luck with *your* crisis, okay?" Jack points his gun in her direction and cocks the trigger.

Lauren screams, and Jack stares her down, saying, "Lauren, I have killed two people since midnight. I have not slept for over twenty-four hours. So maybe ... maybe you should be a little more afraid of me than you are right now."

I think the show's writers should win an Emmy based solely on that two-line dialogue between Lauren and Jack. What a classic! Week after week we intently and intensely watch Jack Bauer face problem after problem. We watch with awe as he escapes incredible dangers. We cheer when he debunks CTU's top brass and disregards protocol to get things done. Adrenaline pumps through our bodies with every episode.

>>WHEN THE FINAL CLOCK UPDATE MARKS THE END OF THE [24] HOUR, WE'LL ALL GO BACK AND FACE THE CHALLENGES, PROBLEMS, AND PAIN OF OUR INDIVIDUAL REALITIES.

But this waitress enters Jack's world and simply reminds us of her reality—working the third shift at a hellacious job and a court appearance for a DUI, of which she's guilty. Real problems. No espionage. No moles unrelated to the animal kingdom. No presidential assassination attempts to thwart. Just life. Plain and simple. Well, maybe not so simple. Lauren's problems bring a lot of pain to her life as she makes her way through one day and into another.

> **"The tragedies and trials come down on us and our questions rise heavenward."**

It's easy to lose ourselves—for an hour—in Jack's world. The production and writing of *24* are first class. And we'd be hard pressed to find a more innovative and creative hour on television. But when the final clock update marks the end of the hour, we'll all go back and face the challenges, problems, and pain of our individual realities.

For example, in the last couple months,

- I've participated at three funerals—the ages of those who died: 17, 39, and 72. *Why?*
- Two of our friend's teenagers were in serious car accidents. *Why?*
- Friends received shocking news that their three-year-old daughter has a brain tumor and, without a miracle, will live only a year or two. *Why?*
- A friend recently buckled under the pressure of financial problems. *Why?*
- Friends struggle courageously to care for their aging parents. *Why?*
- A missionary couple in Japan was informed their unborn baby will likely be born with no arms and perhaps short legs—if the baby even survives his own birth. *Why?*

I really don't need to continue, do I? We get the picture. Maybe we want to add our own "Why?" questions to the list. We've sung the melancholy song before. We each have a starring role in the documentary called _____ (name inserted), *This Is Your Life*. The tragedies and trials come down on us and our questions rise heavenward. As they do, are we truly questioning God or accusing him instead? Will we wait for his answer? Or will we find someone else to blame—someone to take the brunt of our anger and frustration?

Too many times I've heard both clergy and laypeople intimate that we don't trust God enough if we ask, "Why?" But if any of them say to us, "Take the example of Job—he never asked why," we can refute that claim! Check out these questions (paraphrased) Job had for God as he sat buried in suffering and grief:

- Why didn't you let me die at birth? (Job 3:11)
- Why do you keep wretched people like me alive? (3:20–22)
- What do you think I'm made of anyway? Stone? Metal? (6:12)
- Why have you made me your target? (7:20)
- Why do you hide your face from me? (13:24)
- Why don't you let me meet you somewhere face-to-face, so I can state my case? (23:3–6)

>>ABUSE, RAPE, MURDER, OR A MILLION OTHER SINFUL ACTS AREN'T GOD'S WILL. SIN IS *NEVER* GOD'S WILL.

Questioning isn't wrong, unless those questions lead us to doubt the goodness and the promises of God. Questioning the Lord can lead us either toward searching out his ways and truths, or further away from his presence. Questioning while trusting is the key—trusting completely his desire and his power to make all life's tragedies and trials result in some kind of good. Don't underestimate the power of that key—questioning while trusting—to open up peace despite our questions. Don't believe that "everything happens for a reason." Abuse, rape, murder, or a million other sinful acts aren't God's will. Sin is *never* God's will. The truth lies in God's message that he will work for the good of those who love him.

> **""We even put a 'GUILT: Ask for It by Shame' bumper sticker on our car."**

You know, we may not learn the answers to our questions until we arrive in heaven—although then it won't matter to us because we'll be in the perfect presence of our Savior, trusting him perfectly. So listen for and search out answers while trusting.

A major problem with listening and searching for answers while trusting our Savior stems from the built-in *Why-chromosome* in our DNA (Demanding No-nonsense Answers). We demand no-nonsense, immediate answers to our questions, even feeling we have a *right* to know them. We may enjoy a good mystery novel or a suspense-thriller on TV, but we can't stand mysteries in our lives. We want to pinpoint reasons for the problems we face. Obviously, we sometimes *can* pinpoint them, since they're often the consequences of our sin or the result of actions or words we can't take back. Then we don't need to ask—the answer lies in front of us.

Our overactive Why-chromosomes also search out justification, absolution, or maybe just escape from guilt when we realize we're the problem. Guilt, an odd bedfellow, loves to lie around with our unanswered (and our answered) questions. We sleep with it (or at least we try to sleep). We wake up with guilt by our side. Guilt follows us around like a stalker studying his victim. And the cycle seems to continue day in and day out. We even put a "GUILT: Ask for It by Shame" bumper sticker on our cars.

>>IN HIS PERFECT WORLD THERE WERE NO *WHY-CHROMOSOMES*.

Guilt happens ... daily. So does anger. Hopelessness. Stress. Pain. Anxiety. Depression. Grief. Shame. Blame. That's the cycle. *Why?* To answer that one-word question, we look to the genesis of Genesis, where we'll also find the genesis of all our problems. In the genesis, the beginning, God created Adam and Eve along with the first chromosomes. In his perfect world there existed no Why-chromosomes. None of the garbage we deal with daily. Imagine life without _____ (*fill in the blank*). Adam and Eve had the perfect life and relationship. They never had aching sinuses, aching heads, or aching backs. They didn't have to worry about mortgages, 401(k) plans, or debt. No need for the pink drink, anti-diarrhea pills, or PMS meds. No cancer, no surgeries, and even no death. They had none of that ... until they began another chapter in their lives—the third chapter. The third chapter of Genesis explains the genesis of all our problems.

> **"When sin rolled into the world, it brought with it a convoy of Jack Bauer–sized troubles, Lauren-sized difficulties, and our-sized problems."**

The third chapter introduces the Why-chromosome into the world. Its genesis came when the perfect white teeth of the first couple sank into the forbidden fruit of a tree in the middle of their God-created garden home. Enter shame, guilt, worry, sickness, and death—to name just a few problems that now permeate our personal worlds.

I know it sounds so simple. I know it's not the answer we may want. But the genesis of all our problems is (drumroll, please) ... sin. When sin rolled into the world, it brought with it a convoy of Jack Bauer–sized troubles, Lauren-sized difficulties, and our-sized problems. Perfection is a thing of the past. It died when death walked into the world.

> **"And we know that in all things God works for the good of those who love him, who have been called according to his purpose."**
> —Romans 8:28

The end of each hour of the longest day in Jack Bauer's life leaves us wanting more. The weekly cliff-hanger keeps us longing to see what happens next. It gives us plenty to talk about with other *24* addicts.

Maybe today felt like the longest day of your life. I'm not the least bit tempted to leave you with a cliff-hanger, with the hopelessness of the law threatening to push you over the edge. You have to know there's more. The promise of a Savior. Yes, it's right there in Genesis 3, immediately after the announcement of suffering, troubles, and death (see v. 15). With the saving announcement, the Savior rolls in with an even bigger hope and help-filled convoy to get us through the rough times and to create good from the difficulties.

This ending is meant to leave us all wanting more, not just curiously wondering what will happen next, but certain of the joy the future promises. It keeps us longing to see what happens by pointing us in the direction of heaven. Perfection may be a thing of the past, but it's also a thing of the future. We'll have plenty to talk about with others following the story line—Christ's story line and ours that has no ending.

So while the genesis of every possible problem in the world is sin, it's spiritually and physically healthy to seek God's will and his help in every situation as the genesis of our hope. And when the whys arise, run to the Wise One. When guilt raises its ugly head, destroy it with joy in God's gift of forgiveness. Fall in trust with our Savior, knowing anything that has or will happen already passed through his mind, and he's there, around the corner, waiting with help and hope in even the worst of situations.

> Oh, the depth of the riches of the wisdom and knowl-
>   edge of God!
> How unsearchable his judgments,
> and his paths beyond tracing out!
> "Who has known the mind of the Lord?
> Or who has been his counselor?"
> "Who has ever given to God,
> that God should repay him?"
> For from him and through him and to him are all
>   things.
> To him be the glory forever! Amen. (Rom. 11:33–36)

A Master's Degree in Communication Speaks Volumes

We have two ears and one mouth so that we can listen twice as much as we speak.
—Epictetus

Teri, I'm going to find you. I promise.

I know you will.

—Jack and Teri sharing reassurances through their cell phones

>>So don't forget, I'm coming to get you.
—Jack Bauer speaking to his wife and daughter,
via cell phone as he searches for their location
in order to rescue them

>>Jack doesn't seem to have a prayer.

Jack's decked out in a new wardrobe of equipment perfectly fitting for a man on the lam. Fittingly, the LAPD has decked out roadblocks north, south, east, and west in black-and-white wrappers.

>>Jack doesn't seem to have a prayer.

Nina sits in charge of communications. Cell phone in hand, she studies her computer and, with its help, deftly maneuvers Jack out of the city toward Teri and Kim's remote location. Moving cautiously yet desperately, Jack narrowly escapes the net of cops waiting to make him their catch of the day.

Out of the blue, sirens blare. Two uniforms recognize Jack's car and pull him over.

>>Jack doesn't seem to have a prayer.

With the cops mere feet from his car window, tires squeal as Jack peels out. The policemen hustle back to their cars while Jack looks for an escape route. The shrill sirens of backup police cars blast throughout the area. Trapped, Jack tears into a parking lot, jumps out of the car, and cautiously dodges between vehicles, clasping his metal CTU kit firmly. As police scour the area, Jack takes cover under an SUV.

>>Jack doesn't seem to have a prayer.

At the compound, Teri lifts a cell phone from one of Gaines' thugs. Kim takes guard duty. Teri calls CTU. Jack and Nina have already connected on another line. A simple phone patch allows Jack and Teri to talk directly. Hearing Teri's soft voice, Jack reveals an uncharacteristically emotional side of his nothing-rattles-me outer facade. Lying on the ground and hiding from certain arrest, Jack whispers lovingly in Teri's ear via his cold,

>>EVERYTHING WAS AGAINST THEM. THANKFULLY, WE KNEW THAT NOT EVERY*ONE* WAS AGAINST THEM.

inanimate cell phone. He begins with words of remorse for not always being there for Teri when she's needed him. Knowing his family faces grave danger, Jack shares, "I want both of you to know that I'm here for you now, and I love you more than anything in the whole world. I promise you I'm going to get you both out of there, okay? So whatever happens, don't give up. We're a family—we're going to get through this like a family. Okay? So, don't forget, I'm coming to get you."

>>Jack doesn't seem to have a prayer ... but that's nothing new.

The seven young men seated around us didn't seem to have a prayer. In their minds, that condition was probably nothing new. So we prayed for them and with them.

The gymnasium lacked windows, but the heat and humidity found their way in between the clay bricks. Unfortunately, cooling fans didn't find their way in. Sweat dripped from my head as I talked to these seven young men who ranged in age from sixteen to twenty-one. My partner and I sat in white plastic chairs trying to convince these men they did have a prayer, even though they felt convinced they didn't. In all honesty, my mind took some punches at my heart, trying to convince *me,* too, that they really did have a prayer. I wanted to believe that. Everything was against them. Thankfully, we knew that not every*one* was against them.

> **"They were well acquainted with the imaginary revolving door which led them easily in and out and in and out of prison."**

We sat in the gym, listening to their stories. We talked. We listened. We talked. We prayed. We listened. The seven young men sat in street clothes, yet they were in prison—their holding place until their cases went to trial. Their alleged crimes included dealing and abusing drugs, robbery, and even rape. They were well acquainted with the imaginary revolving door which led them easily in and out and in and out of prison. The group included second-, third-, and even fourth-time offenders. They truly didn't seem to have a prayer. They knew only the hard, criminal lifestyle—both in and out of prison. Their friends and family had little or nothing ... except for the drugs that kept them high from day to day. They'd steal to feed their habit. They'd lie, cheat, and beg to make it through a day. They'd even kill if they had to.

The prison and its inmates sat in a dark, poverty-stricken part of the world. As part of a mission team, we came to the prison with listening ears and the good news that these men did have a prayer ... along with One to whom they could pray. After our leaders shared with the prisoners-in-waiting, we divided up into small groups to visit. Our teams were made up of one man and one woman. My partner had walked through dark times in her life before the Life-giver taught her what real living was all about. She shared her story—his story in her life—and the prisoners connected with her past way of life. I shared about growing up without a father and about learning forgiveness from a death row inmate to whom I once ministered. Some of the prisoners talked freely, while some spoke only if you spoke to them.

>> THEIR HOPE FOR A FUTURE, OR LACK OF HOPE, WEIGHED ON MY HEART.

Their hope for a future, or lack of hope, weighed on my heart. Sure, we shared hope through Christ—his promises and presence—but I knew that when released from prison, someday they would walk right back into a home, neighborhood, and friends that imprisoned them just as surely as the walls within which they now lived. Did they have a prayer?

As I said, we prayed with them and for them. After spending quite some time with them, our group waited for transportation back to our mission post. As we did so, their conversation with us became more casual. Unfortunately, their talk then focused on my partner, an attractive young woman in her midtwenties. The conversation obviously headed in the wrong direction. You need to know that this lady holds nothing back, will speak her mind, and tells it like it is. She stood her ground as their talk turned inappropriate. Just before we left, the comments of a twenty-one-year-old prisoner took an unacceptable turn. As we turned to leave, he came over to her, seemingly apologetic. He asked her to pray with him. She placed her hand on one shoulder, and I placed mine on the other. She began to pray.

> **"Lord, smack this guy across his face!"**

"Lord, smack this guy across his face!" she said, forcefully and sincerely. Now this was a prayer like no other *I'd* ever prayed. I opened my eyes, looked at her, and thought to myself, "Did I hear that right?" She continued to pray for this young man who seemingly didn't have a prayer. She prayed that he would wake up to the love of a Savior who offers a life full of gifts to help grow and enrich his life.

> **"She continued to pray for this young man who seemingly didn't have a prayer."**

I don't think her prayer's slappin' request offended God, or the man either, for that matter. He knew he was out of line. My partner's prayer reminded his mind and spirit that a loving, spiritual whack upside of the head might do him some good as he moved beyond the prison walls and out into the world.

I must admit, her prayer's beginning still makes me smile. And it also reminds me that I need a good face and faith smackin' from the Lord every so often.

The I've-got-a-hopeless-future blues have an easy-to-follow melody line. It's one of those tunes that's hard to get out of your mind. Many times I've whined and cried that I don't have a prayer. How 'bout you?

>> I NEED A GOOD FACE AND FAITH SMACKIN' FROM THE LORD EVERY SO OFTEN.

Ever felt like you haven't got a prayer when ...

- the amount on the bill doesn't come close to the amount in your account?

- love seems to have walked past your open door?
- you're in a rut the size of the Grand Canyon?
- the pull of the temptation knocks you off your feet?
- poverty, unemployment, and ungodliness hang out at every corner of your neighborhood?
- your "prisons" have a revolving door custom-made especially for you?

> **"Even when you don't know what to pray, the Holy Spirit takes your wordless sighs and aching groans and shapes them into perfect prayers [see Rom. 8:26 MSG]."**

We do have a prayer, you know. No matter the situation. No matter if we don't know what to pray for or how to pray. No matter if we've never prayed before. We have a prayer, and we have One who hears our prayers. He loves to sit across from us and tell us his story. It's the most incredible, life-changing testimony we'll ever hear. He can relate to what we're going through. He's been there and has come back to help and rescue us.

Talk. Don't hold back. He can take it. He urges you to tell him exactly what's on your mind—detail by gory detail. Bold prayers won't offend him. And even when you don't know what to pray, the Holy Spirit takes your wordless sighs and aching groans and shapes them into perfect prayers (see Rom. 8:26 MSG).

True enough, our situations may seem hopeless. We may feel we don't have a prayer. But even in the worst scenario, hope comes in the form of Jesus. If we have nothing else to hold on to except receiving our Savior's gift of heaven, then let's hold on to that truth. If you're stuck in a place that doesn't offer an escape, Jesus wants to communicate his life hope right now. Even when living in hopeless situations on earth, you have heaven's hopeful answer. Things won't always be this bleak. You have his word on it. Heaven is the answer to creation's cry for liberation.

Interestingly, Jack Bauer's words to his wife and daughter seem similar to ones Jesus might whisper in our ears. We'd hear, "I want you to know that I'm here for you now, and I love you more than anything in the whole world. I promise you I'm going to get you out of there, okay? So whatever happens, don't give up. We're a family—we're going to get through this like a family. Okay? So don't forget, I'm coming to get you."

> Meanwhile, the moment we get tired in the waiting, God's Spirit is right alongside helping us along. If we don't know how or what to pray, it doesn't matter. He does our praying in and for us, making prayer out of our wordless sighs, our aching groans. He knows us far better than we know ourselves, knows our pregnant condition, and keeps us present before God. That's why we can be so sure that every detail in our lives of love for God is worked into something good. (Rom. 8:26–28 MSG)

Losing Control Brings Everything Under Control

I have been crucified with Christ
and I no longer live, but
Christ lives in me.

—Galatians 2:20

>>This is personal ...
—Jack Bauer, realizing what
lies behind the attempt to
kill him, his family, and
Senator Palmer

Crucified on Calv'ry's mountain, I find life, although I die
With my sins, my life, my wisdom, sinful will and all I own.
Here I nail them, with my Savior. With Christ crucified, I die.
But the life I live in body, I will live by faith alone.

Black leather and instrument panels surround Jack Bauer. Hiding behind sunglasses and an unfazed gaze, the determined agent poses as a chauffeur in order to move a step closer in his quest to find and rescue his abducted wife and daughter. His expected passenger is Kevin Carroll. Using the driver's side mirror, Jack spots Carroll approaching the rear of the limousine. As his passenger comes to within a few steps of the car, Jack recognizes him as the man with Teri at the hospital, the one who called himself Alan York. When Carroll/York climbs in the back, Jack locks the doors and slowly turns to face the con man behind him. Carroll draws his gun and shoots repeatedly. The partition between the seats is bulletproof, and bullets aimed directly at Jack's face ricochet off it. Jack doesn't flinch. He peels out of the garage and drives in wild zigzags, tossing Carroll around the back seat. Carroll's head slams into the partition as Jack slams on the brakes. Jack jumps out of the car and yanks Carroll out of the back seat, demanding to know the whereabouts of his family.

While Jack appears to be in control of the situation, Carroll holds the answer Bauer needs. An agreement is made. Jack will allow Carroll to leave unharmed only if Carroll directs him to the Gaines compound where Teri and Kim are hostages. The control issue plays like a game. Jack controls Kevin Carroll's fate, while Carroll controls Jack's ability to find his family.

A solid sheet of ice surrounded me. There I sat—in the middle of a field of ice spread over acres. Thankfully I wasn't alone. The "master" sat beside me. He had the credentials. I knew I could trust him, but fear caused my apprehension to climb. I gripped firmly at the ten-and-two positions, as instructed. My mind called me, "Fool!" The one next to me called me to task. I took a deep breath and floored it. Ten. Twenty. Thirty. Forty. Fifty miles an hour. "Now! Slam on the brakes!" the undaunted passenger yelled to me. I followed his command.

Immediately I lost control of the car as the front end skidded hard to the left on the field of ice. The passenger remained silent, watching for my reaction. I remembered the lesson. Turn *into* the skid. That made no sense to me, but my heart told me to trust the lesson and the teacher. I let off the accelerator and steered into the

> **"If I had just turned against what reason told me, things would have come under control."**

skid. Unbelievable! It worked. The car straightened out! This fact pleased the driver's ed teacher, a former race car driver, sitting next to me. I'm glad I trusted this "master" who taught me about spinning out of control.

On the other hand, I wish I had trusted *The Master* so many more times when my life spun out of control. If I had just turned against what reason told me, things would have come under control. It shouldn't be difficult to trust *The Master's* teachings, but we rationalize it's easier to turn with the direction of the wheels that spin in our minds, even if they spin out of control. Maybe we feel in control when we flow with what is actually out of control.

Check out these *Master-full* words as we consider trusting him. "I have been crucified with Christ and I no longer live, but Christ lives in me. The life I live in the body, I live by faith in the Son of God, who loved me and gave himself for me" (Gal. 2:20).

Wait a minute. Crucified with Christ? Things are definitely out of control! Crucifixion equals death. If I don't steer away from death, my mind will call out, "Fool!" Right?

> **❝When I start to skid out of control, I give up the control that reason has over me.❞**

The brakes squeal. *What? I no longer live?* That goes against all reason. It fatally pierces my ego. Those words steer me in another direction—away from God.

But before I go too far, I think again. Christ lives in me? So I'm still here—flesh and bones—but, *the life I live in the body, I live by faith in the Son of God, who loved me and gave himself for me.* I'm here walking around, but I'm living by faith as Christ lives in me and through me. Sounds like I'm letting Christ take the lead. When I start to skid out of control, I give up the control reason has over me. With Christ's help I turn against the way my life is going and turn toward God, following his ways and words—allowing his will to live in me. I don't want to do it as some kind of lucky charm—only when things are going badly. It's a constant. It's a faith issue. I can live freely with Christ in control.

>>IN MANY WAYS I'VE BEEN *BLESSED* WITH DEPRESSION.

When I lose control and turn toward Christ, who lives in me, then I realize he has everything under control. Losing control to gain control. Interesting. Challenging. My mind finds that difficult to comprehend. Faith has to take over and my will take a back seat.

> **❝God doesn't use some divine robotic buttons for control.❞**

I know God doesn't use some divine robotic buttons for control. He's given me free will to make certain choices. I realize the unconditional love he has for me, and that he gave his life so I could learn what real living is all about. Steering in his direction, by the help of and power of the Holy Spirit, only makes sense. My faith grabs on to that concept—that gift—but my human mind struggles with it sometimes.

>>HE WASN'T JUST SITTING NEXT TO ME, HE HAD COME TO *LIVE* WITHIN ME!

I mentioned in an early chapter that I've dealt with depression. I still deal with it, or at least I'm still on medication. I realize it's a part of who I am—at least in this chapter of my life. In many ways I've been *blessed* with depression. It has opened new ways to minister I never considered before.

God turned my life *into* the skid instead of letting it continue to spin out of control. Some of my ability to cope came through medication; through caring, praying Christian friends and family; and through the presence and promises of Christ. Thankfully, God always kept a window of grace open, letting some light into my dark world. I'm grateful for that gift.

> "Abraham and Sarah served as cochairs of the Canaan Chapter of AARP."

You see, even when I couldn't turn toward the skid—into it—not only was my Master-Savior present to help turn the wheel, but he sent others to help steer my out-of-control life in the direction of safety and stability. He wasn't just sitting next to me, he had come to *live* within me! Losing control and letting God and his gifts steer me into the skid, everything was under control. What a unique faith truth from a creative God!

Abraham—not the one from the land of Lincoln, rather the one from the land of Ur—learned a similar lesson while he drove ... cattle, not a car. Abraham and his wife, Sarah—not the Plain and Tall one of book fame but the beautiful one of biblical fame—wanted a child desperately. But the couple seemed infertile. It's one thing to say Sarah's (known as Sarai at that time) biological clock was ticking ... her clock's alarm had gone off! She spent her days hitting the snooze button over and over. Abraham and Sarah served as cochairs of the Canaan Chapter of AARP.

The amazing part of this story is a pledge the Lord gave to Abraham and Sarah. When Abraham was seventy-five, the Lord promises them not only a child, but descendants as numerous as the stars in the sky. Abraham squints (where *had* he put those magnifiers?) into the night sky, and he stands there, in awe of the unfathomable number of stars above him, as God makes his promise. So he and Sarah wait. No morning sickness. Mourning, she is sick of the infertility. The Early Pregnancy Test strips don't turn blue.

> **"What's causing the rubber to hit the ice patches in your life?"**

Finally, at age eighty-five, Abraham figures God's way isn't working; so, at the encouragement of Sarah, Abraham sleeps with Hagar, Sarah's maidservant. Obviously the infertility problem isn't due to Abraham's low sperm count, because Hagar gives birth to a son. They give him the name Ishmael.

Abraham thought he took control. By doing things his way, his dream of having a son came true. But God's plan differed from that of Abraham and Sarah. With conflict brewing on the home front, Hagar and Ishmael were sent away. Abraham lost control of his life and finally turned it over to God's control. Then God made sure everything came under control. Twenty-five years after God's promise, Sarah gave birth to a son, by Abraham, just as God had promised.

Womb for a miracle. That's what Sarah had. They named the miracle Isaac.

What's your story? Are you involved in a life-and-death struggle for control, like Jack Bauer and Kevin Carroll, and looking for an important ally? What's causing the rubber to hit the ice patches in your life? A prodigal child? Loneliness? Bill collectors? Addictions? Feelings of worthlessness? Bitterness? Lack of direction or purpose? Work troubles? Home problems? What is it?

We don't have the energy or strength to turn the steering wheels of our own lives, do we? Instead, let's allow Christ—who lives within us—to turn our spinning, out-of-control lives into the skid—toward God's stabilizing love, forgiveness, and strength. When spiritually losing control of our self-focused lives and giving them to Jesus Christ, we find he brings everything under control. Do we have room for that miracle in our lives? It's conceivable. God has named the miracle Grace.

>>Dear Master,
>>Savior of my out-of-control life, you desire and deserve all of me, so take my heart, Lord, take it. Let my old way of life be crucified with you and I will live by faith, responding to your love for me. Comforted by your peaceful stability, I fall in love with you all over again.

You Deserve All of Me

Holy God of love
Who lives inside my heart
Author of the galaxy
I want to know Your ways
I want to feel Your every heartbeat
But more than I want You
You want me

You deserve all of me
So take my heart, Lord, take it
You deserve all of me
So take my life, Lord, take it
You're the One who is exalted
You're the One who set me free
Lord Jesus, I give all—I give all of me

Don't want to be conformed
To the pattern of this world
I want to be transformed by You
So Lord renew my mind
And let Your thoughts consume me
Till all that's left of me is You[1]

Not Everyone Is in the Dark

But me, I'm not giving up.
I'm sticking around to see what God will do.
I'm waiting for God to make things right.
I'm counting on God to listen to me.

Don't, enemy, crow over me.
I'm down, but I'm not out.
I'm sitting in the dark right now,
but God is my light.
—Micah 7:7–8 (MSG)

What's Jack doing, Tony?

*—CTU District Agent
Alberta Green,
interrogating Tony about
Bauer's whereabouts*

>>Jack Bauer: My wife and daughter are in one of these buildings. Which one?

>>Kevin Carroll: I don't know.

>>Bauer (*agitated*): Take a guess.

—Conversation in which Jack threatens Kevin Carroll's life to learn the location of his family

Jack's eyes. His eyes tell the story of intense hours, a sleepless night, and a deep desire to find his wife and daughter. Frustration boils behind the whites of his eyes. Cliché or not, Jack Bauer isn't used to being left in the dark. Jack Bauer doesn't like losing control.

He's close. He knows it.

>>Don't play dumb, Carroll. Which building? You
know where they are, scum.

>>I don't know.

His nervous trigger finger and twitching eye bore holes through Carroll's head as Jack accentuates the three syllables using his I'm-not-joking-around voice, "Take a guess!"

At the same time, unknowingly not far from Jack, Teri and Kim make a run for it. At least that's the plan.

As they gather the confidence to run, they hear someone entering their makeshift prison. Teri nervously but steadily grasps her weapon, bracing herself to meet the threat she can hear but not see around the corner. A highly trained professional, arm outstretched with gun poised, whips his body around the corner, and Jack finds Teri his unsuspecting target. He grabs her, making sure she doesn't scream. His grip slowly loosens and turns into an embrace. The three are no longer left in the dark—they've found each other and emotion overcomes them.

Reflecting last weekend on the cliché "left in the dark," I realized I'm in the dark about a lot of things. Hospice care began for a seventy-year-old friend yesterday. His family is left in the dark about when he'll enter heaven. I met a couple today who are keeping their friends and family in the dark that they're getting married. They've invited their guests to a banquet hall for an engagement party. Little do the guests know (except for the couple's parents) the engagement party is actually a wedding ceremony.

> **"Have you been left in the dark, uncertain if the downsizing will affect your job?"**

The due date for my nephew and his wife's first baby is a month away. Everyone is in the dark as to the exact date ... until today, when their daughter comes a month early.

My wife's birthday is this week. She's in the dark about the presents I'll give her (because I'm still in the dark about what I'm getting her).

My oldest son just left for college (eleven hours away). I was left in the dark about just how difficult his leaving would be for me.

I'm left in the dark about how much money my wife and daughter spent shopping today. I'll have to be surprised when the credit card bill comes.

Until I gave it some thought, I didn't realize how often I'm left in the dark. What about you? Have you been left in the dark,

- wondering when—or if—you'll get a raise;
- hoping, but not knowing if the insurance will cover the damage;
- questioning if your decision about your child will affect his/her future;
- unsure if you can stay away from pornography another day;
- uncertain if the downsizing will affect your job;

- doubting, while hoping, your family will get along at the next get-together;
- wondering if you'll go on a date in the next few weeks;
- curious if you'll make it home without breaking down;
- not knowing if you'll have the money to make the next car payment?

> **"So many questions. So few answers."**

So many questions; so few answers ... at least for now. We're uncomfortable left in the dark. We need that familiar control.

Maybe you've heard the old story about Cleo and Simon. These friends often took walks together. Their favorite route took them about seven miles into town ... and, of course, seven miles back home.

One particular afternoon their legs didn't feel very spry. They seem to bear the weight of the world on their shoulders. Despite the black cloud hanging over their heads like a caricature, they talk as usual, each intellectually inspiring the other. This day's discussion bears a particularly heavy topic.

Cleo and Simon are so lost in their exchange they don't realize a man catches up with them on the road. Cleo and Simon, while not being rude, keep their focus on the topic at hand. Intrigued, the man interrupts, asking what they are talking about. He can see the two are upset, and he doesn't want to be left in the dark. Cleo can't believe the man is in the dark about it. Had the man been sleeping under a rock all weekend? Cleo tells him how a popular young preacher was murdered—publicly and right along the street. People watched and did nothing to help—maybe they were scared of the gang who killed him. To make matters worse, this morning reports came out that some sick people actually stole his body from the grave. How could anyone do that? Why would anyone want to disturb the remains of this man of peace? So many questions. So few answers.

The unknown walker who broke into their conversation stops suddenly, leading Cleo and Simon to stop, as well. They can't help noticing the shocked, even disgusted, look on his face. The man seems shocked they don't know what really happened. He goes so far as to call them foolish! Then he proceeds to enlighten them. The man explains that they should have known this was going to happen. Predictions of this incident had surfaced some time ago.

>> HE NOT ONLY KNOWS ABOUT THE STORY, BUT, LIKE A PULITZER PRIZE—WINNING INVESTIGATIVE REPORTER, THIS MAN KNOWS ALL THE DETAILS *BEHIND* THE STORY.

The man obviously *hadn't* spent the weekend under a rock. He isn't in the dark at all. He not only knows *about* the story, but, like a Pulitzer Prize–winning investigative reporter, this man knows all the details *behind* the story. Without looking at notes, he begins at the beginning and explains every detail of the story to the present. The man sheds light on the details surrounding the murder and the misinformation about the missing body. He doesn't want them to remain in the dark about the murdered man's story.

Time passes more quickly today than any other time they walk this seven-mile stretch of road. The sun begins its descent. Their stomachs growl. Their home lies just ahead. As they turn down their street, the man continues walking. Cleo and Simon stop him and insist he stay, since it is getting late. Food waits at the end of their cul-de-sac. Placing an extra chair at the dinner table isn't a problem. The man accepts the invitation.

When the three sit to eat, their guest offers a blessing. He picks up the fresh bread, gives thanks to God, breaks it, and hands it to the others. The men almost drop the bread as well as their jaws. This is no ordinary meal. This is no ordinary man. They are sitting in the presence of the same pastor the Romans had murdered a few days earlier. Obviously, nobody stole his body. Rather, this man steals their hearts. Before his name could roll off their lips, the man disappears. The man they first thought had spent the weekend under a rock, actually did! Under a rock, inside a rock tomb hewed into the side of a hill. He certainly is a *man of the cloth* like no other—he left his burial cloths as a calling card announcing he was the Risen Savior!

> **"This is no ordinary meal. This is no ordinary man."**

>>HE CERTAINLY IS A *MAN OF THE CLOTH* LIKE NO OTHER—HE LEFT HIS BURIAL CLOTHS AS A CALLING CARD ANNOUNCING HE WAS THE RISEN SAVIOR!

When they finally compose themselves, Cleo (Cleopas) and his walking partner asks over and over, "Were not our hearts burning within us while he talked with us on the road and opened the Scriptures to us?" (Luke 24:32). So many emotions! Jesus had shone light on the darkness of their misinformation and the darkness in their lives, enlightening them not only about his death and resurrection, but also about how all of Scripture—from Moses through the prophets—pointed to this Messiah, *the* Messiah.

They can hardly believe all they'd missed even while diligently reading and studying what we know as the Old Testament. This dead man walking, the promised Messiah, fulfilled all the prophecies about him. He was the ...

- Passover lamb (Ex. 12)
- Sin-carrying scapegoat (Lev. 16)
- Year of Jubilee in skin and bones (Lev. 25:6–55)
- One who lived (and spoke) the words of Psalm 22
- Child born for us—called Wonderful Counselor, Mighty God, Everlasting Father, the Prince of Peace (Isa. 9:6)
- Suffering servant (Isa. 49–56)
- Palm Sunday king riding on a donkey, on a colt, the foal of a donkey (Zech. 9:9)
- ... And so much more!

Along the Emmaus road (see Luke 24:13–35), two followers of Jesus walked (figuratively) in the dark about the full, true meaning of the Scriptures. After they walked with Jesus, they would continue to walk in the light, with the Light. Well, except for

> **"What we're in the dark about, Jesus sees in the light."**

that night. They don't walk, they hurry back down the seven-mile road from Emmaus to Jerusalem. They can't wait to tell the disciples and their friends, still in the dark about the weekend events. They come shouting, "It is true! The Lord has risen" (Luke 24:33–35). They relay the events— every one of them—about how a *perfect* stranger (literally) had talked with them, how he explained Scripture to them, and how they finally recognized him when he broke the bread at their table.

Light flooded into a room of people in the dark. Their world had changed dramatically with the dark news of his death and again even more with the bright news of his resurrection.

The Gospels tell us that as Jesus hung on the cross, darkness came over the whole land (see Luke 23:44–45). Jesus died in the dark but didn't leave us in the dark.

We may think God hides the answers to all our questions from us. True, some things haven't been revealed. We don't have all the answers. That's okay, friends. Since Jesus reveals himself to us, we walk in the light, with *the* Light. We anticipate and praise God for allowing the light of his Word to work as a bright beam of clarity showing us how to live, where we should go, and when is the right time to make decisions. That may sound too simplistic or implausible, but the more time we spend in the light of the Lord, the more intimately we'll know him and his ways. We'll discover he truly wants to share his will and wisdom with us.

What we're in the dark about, Jesus sees in the light. Is that why the apostle Paul could say, "I have learned the secret of being content in any and every situation" (Phil. 4:12)? Paul wasn't in the dark anymore. He just trusted *the* Light.

No doubt Paul's heart also felt ablaze with light when God revealed the Scriptures to him. Contentment comes to us, too, as we open Scripture while the Holy Spirit opens our faith to understanding it and trusting it. Hearts ablaze with the resurrection news reflect the light of Jesus' love and salvation, his example and forgiveness. Jesus truly doesn't want us to be left walking in the dark. He came to shine his light on our darkness, to walk with us, and to stay with us.

Claim Responsibility, Not Injustice

Make a careful exploration of who you are and the work you have been given, and then sink yourself into that. Don't be impressed with yourself. Don't compare yourself with others. Each of you must take responsibility for doing the creative best you can with your own life.
—Galatians 6:4–5 (MSG)

How can I do the job when my own house isn't in order?

—Presidential candidate David Palmer

>>Some part of getting a second chance is taking responsibility for the mess you made in the first place. You understand me?
—Jack Bauer to Rick as they hide out in a water tower

Teri Bauer's eyes widen in alarm.

Something–something *big*–just exploded. You can almost see the thoughts racing through her head.

>>Was that Jack? After all we've been through,
       after all he did to rescue us from Gaines and
                  his crew of terrorist kidnappers,
                        did they kill him after all?

The sight of Kim, running through the wilderness beside her, is enough to bring her back to the task at hand.

They are running. Jack has come and, with the help of their repentant kidnapper, Rick, managed to free them all from the building that held them prisoner. Now they must get to safety–to an abandoned water tower–where they can hide from Gaines' thugs until reinforcements arrive.

If it's not too late already ...

Teri Bauer's eyes are still wide as they rove across the wooded spaces before them. The eyes speak fear, though she's trying to hide it from her daughter. Are they lost? Shouldn't they have reached the rendezvous spot by now? She blinks, willing herself to focus, and yet something is going terribly wrong.

>>Where is that water tower?

A few hundred yards away, Jack Bauer and Rick-the-reformed-kidnapper tumble into the water tower. It's empty. Teri and Kim should be there. But it's empty.

Jack's eyes flash with determination, taking in the situation.

Rick is wounded, bleeding where a bullet from one of Gaines' men struck him in the arm. The boy wanted to quit, wanted to surrender, wanted to give in to the pain—and maybe to the guilt—he felt. But Jack Bauer is a force to be reckoned with, and when he refuses to let you quit, well, you just don't quit.

It was Jack who had realized their only chance of escape was to cut the gas line on the van that was their temporary protection from Gaines' men. With a precision that comes from practice, he had rolled under the van, cut the line, and rolled out again in a heartbeat. Pulling Rick after him, he'd moved them to a safe spot, then turned and fired at the van. The resulting explosion was deafening—and enough of a distraction to allow an opportunity for escape to safety; escape to the water tower where they could meet up with Teri and Kim and hide.

And now, in the water tower, Jack's brow furrows. Teri and Kim should have been here by now.

>>Where are they?

Finally finding a moment to breathe, hiding in this tower cave, Jack winds a cloth tourniquet around Rick's arm, hoping it will stop the bleeding. Kneeling at Rick's side, playing nursemaid—one tough nurse-maid at that—he intuitively catches Rick's remorseful look.

"Some part of getting a second chance," he says in a low voice, "is taking responsibility for the mess you made in the first place." He locks eyes with the injured boy. "You understand me?"

And in this moment, amidst the explosions and gunfire and shouts from the outside, the inside of this water tower echoes the silence of a call for responsibility, not a claim of injustice.

Watered-down lawsuits claim injustice, not responsibility. Listen for the polluted raindrops falling from these supposedly true lawsuits:

- A woman was awarded $780,000 by a jury after breaking her ankle tripping over a child running around a furniture store. The store owners were understandably shocked at the verdict, considering the unruly toddler was her own son.

- A jury awarded a teenager $74,000 and medical expenses when his neighbor ran over his hand with a car. The teen apparently didn't notice there was someone at the wheel of the car as he worked to steal his neighbor's hubcaps.

- A college student decided to "moon" someone from his fourth-story dorm room window. He lost his balance, fell out of his window, and injured himself. He filed a suit against the university for "not warning him of the dangers of living on the fourth floor."

Where's Jack Bauer when you need him? Tell 'em, Jack: "Some part of getting a second chance is taking responsibility for the mess you made in the first place." Jack needs to lock eyes with the lady wearing an ankle cast, the hubcap crook, and the student singing "Moon River," and say, *"You understand me?"*

> **"Inside of this water tower echoes the silence of a call for responsibility, not a claim of injustice."**

Most claims of injustice don't make the news, but they do hit home. My son Benjamin and his friend Adam were coloring one day. They had just learned to write their own names. At one point, my son came to us accusing his friend of writing on the wall. Adam defended himself, accusing Benjamin of doing it. They played the blame game back and forth for a while until my wife and I went into the room. It didn't take Jack Bauer to detect the guilty party, because he left his calling card on the wall. It read *Adam* (with his signature *d* written backward).

That's a simplistic case in point. We all have plenty of examples where the writing is on the wall, so to speak, reminding us there's a need to hear the call to take responsibility, not simply claim injustice.

Check out two more accounts from the halls of *justice* (?):

A governor pulled this one off. The execution date had

> **"He couldn't take the responsibility, so he decided not to issue a decision."**

been set for a man many thought was innocent of any wrongdoing. Appeals had been denied and execution would take place within hours. There was still hope of the governor granting a pardon. The governor received the plea and held on to it for as long as possible. He didn't know how to respond.

>>WITH GREAT POWER COMES GREAT RESPONSIBILITY.

—UNCLE BEN IN *SPIDER-MAN* THE MOVIE

He had his eyes on a more impressive political career. How would his decision affect his future? How would his constituents react to his verdict—no matter his response? Reports spread about his belief in the innocence of the man, yet his middle name should have been

"Coward." He couldn't take the responsibility, so he decided not to issue a decision. He literally passed the case off and washed his hands of the entire incident. His lack of action allowed the execution to go forward. But no one could point a finger at him, claiming the responsibility for this man's death fell on him. Or so he hoped.

>>ONE WASHED HIS HANDS IN A BASIN OF WATER. THE OTHER COULDN'T WASH HIMSELF, EVEN IF HIS HANDS HADN'T BEEN PINNED TO A CROSS. THE WASHING COULD ONLY COME FROM SOMEONE ELSE.

"Dumb criminals." You've heard or read their stories, I'm sure. This story is one for the ages. A crook spent a Friday afternoon hanging around outside town. Those in law enforcement knew his crime. They had their eye on him. They were milling around him, mixing with the rest of the people that day. Out of the blue this man did something most crooks don't do—he confessed! He opened up—in the presence of God and everybody—and confessed the crime! He gave it up. He spilled the beans. He actually claimed responsibility for his mistake. Law enforcement had him pinned for the crime.

While he knew taking responsibility for his crime would be the death of him, things ended up differently. Maybe his mantra wasn't "dumb criminal" after all. While witnesses figured him a fool, the judge, hearing his confession, declared everything cool. He released the man, giving him the gift of freedom.

Here's another record of those final two accounts that I just shared:

"When Pilate saw that he was getting nowhere, but that instead an uproar was starting, he took water and washed his hands in front of the

crowd. 'I am innocent of this man's blood,' he said. 'It is your responsibility!'" (Matt. 27:24).

"One of the criminals who hung there hurled insults at him: 'Aren't you the Christ? Save yourself and us!'

"But the other criminal rebuked him. 'Don't you fear God,' he said, 'since you are under the same sentence? We are punished justly, for we are getting what our deeds deserve. But this man has done nothing wrong.'

"Then he said, 'Jesus, remember me when you come into your kingdom.'

"Jesus answered him, 'I tell you the truth, today you will be with me in paradise'" (Luke 23:39–43).

> **"It was all his doing; we had nothing to do with it. He gave us a good bath, and we came out of it new people, washed inside and out by the Holy Spirit."**
>
> **—Titus 3:5** MSG

One washed his hands of the situation, unwilling to claim responsibility. One claimed responsibility, and his Savior washed away his sins.

One washed his hands in a basin of water. The other couldn't wash himself, even if his hands hadn't been pinned to a cross. The washing could only come from someone else.

While the Roman law enforcement officers thought the confessing criminal on the cross was a fool, the gospel-giver, sin-washer beside him changed his life as well as his name—from *sinner* to *forgiven*. The blood of Jesus washed him clean of sin—this blood that the repentant thief could see as it formed a puddle at the feet of Jesus.

> In the midst of our difficult situations and complex times, we must take responsibility for our wrong choices. Part of an authentic lament is repentance. There has to be a moment of clarity when we admit that we've

> **❝The sin-washer has a name. That name is Jesus Christ.❞**

violated God's will and shunned his love. This is radical honesty. It is painful, but its genuineness leads us to see God as he really is—in constant pursuit of us. (David Edwards)[1]

The sin-washer has a name. That name is Jesus Christ. He's hanging around us at this very moment. He's in constant pursuit of our hearts. He desperately wants to spend eternity with us. He doesn't live in a barren water tower, but rather his life overflows with a life-giving water that will never dry up.

Care to say anything to him? Our *just* Savior has something to share with us. Don't worry, we won't get what we deserve. He only acts justly and has graciously taken full responsibility for our irresponsible lives.

Go ahead, talk with him—he's ready to listen and respond with his undeserved love.

Really ...

Go ahead.

He's listening.

Legalism Levels Lives

But now a righteousness from God, apart from law, has been made known, to which the Law and the Prophets testify. This righteousness from God comes through faith in Jesus Christ to all who believe. There is no difference, for all have sinned and fall short of the glory of God, and are justified freely by his grace through the redemption that came by Christ Jesus.
—Romans 3:21–24

>>Unfortunately, as you know, our procedures don't allow for any deviation from protocol.... I can't reinstate you, Jack.

—Ryan Chappelle,
CTU Regional Director

She's secure in Jack's arms. Her body relaxes as it leans into his. She can glance into his eyes. Yes, he's real. *Life* is again real. Teri inhales refreshing freedom and wholeness and exhales that polluted air of terror.

> **"Unfortunately, as you know, our procedures don't allow for any deviation from protocol.... I can't reinstate you."**
> **—Ryan Chappelle, CTU Regional Director**

The jarring landing of the helicopter jolts her sense of reality and brings her back to earth. The Bauers hurry out, hunchbacklike, from under the whipping blades of the helicopter. Teri recognizes an uneasy look on Jack's pursed face as he tells his contradictory story of rescue, remorse, and resolution. His words stress the happy ending, but his expression worries her. She realizes she's about to dive into the familiar pool of disconnectedness, twisting with a 9.5 degree of difficulty. Several agents escort Jack into CTU while others escort Teri and Kim in the opposite direction to a medical clinic. One final over-the-shoulder gaze reassures her, as Jack's look tells her everything will be okay.

>>Will my family ever return home—feel any sense of normalcy?

Carried on an adrenaline high for hours, Jack finds himself suddenly grounded by reality's gravity. The unplanned landing strands Bauer in CTU's sterile holding room #2, and he holds a one-way ticket to house arrest.

>>I don't have time for this! Just reinstate me
and let me do my job.

More than a debriefing, an interrogation clock begins to tick when CTU Regional Director Ryan Chappelle carries his confidence over the threshold of holding room #2.

>>Let's make this quick. I had no choice in what
I did. My family's lives were at stake!

Chappelle attempts to steady himself on an emotional balance beam, teetering precariously between his respect for Jack and a bloodthirsty need to find fault in the restless man across the table. The conversation begins with a cordial air that soon turns stale. Seeing Chappelle's all-business attitude and the recorder memorizing his every word, Jack gives a sterile report of the timeline of events in keeping with the sterile environment of the holding room.

>>Terrorists want Palmer dead. My family's
dealing with separation anxiety ... again.
You're killing me with your legalistic crap.

>>Unfortunately, as you know, our procedures
don't allow for any deviation from protocol.... I
can't reinstate you, Jack.

>>It's all black-and-white to you, isn't it? Did
you break all the colors highlighting the 613

laws in your CTU Director's Manual? You may
live by the law, Chappelle—but I live by the
mantra "the ends justify the means."

What actually took place is this: I tried keeping rules
and working my head off to please God, and it didn't
work. So I quit being a "law man" so that I could be
God's man.

—The apostle Paul, Galatians 2:19 (MSG)

Why do so many people find themselves buried alive under a pile
of guilt? Sound familiar? Maybe we've been to a church where, like
a surgeon's scalpel, the law slices into hearts, condemning—as is its
purpose—and allowing little or no gospel (good news) to resuscitate
the broken heart and heal the exit wound of the law's sharp blade.
Sermons. Sunday schools. Bible studies. Misinterpreted Scripture. TV
and radio programs. E-mails. Evangelism visits. Anyone or anything
that leaves us sitting hopelessly in the mire of guilt and the stench of
legalism—all culprits. Those entrenched in legalism can't see how it
affects their faith, relationships (including fellowship with Christ), and
joyless lives.

>> WE TRY TO PLEASE GOD IN
EVERYTHING AND FAIL, LEFT
SPIRITUALLY FRUITLESS AND BROKEN.

Legalism becomes part of our daily routine, our way of life. We try to please God in everything and fail, left spiritually fruitless and broken. Through the cracks in our strong resolve guilt begins to seep in, and before we know it, we're filled with hopelessness. We want to be obedient and strong, but we regularly fail.

> Indeed, I have been crucified with Christ. My ego is no longer central. It is no longer important that I appear righteous before you or have your good opinion, and I am no longer driven to impress God. Christ lives in me.
>
> —The apostle Paul, Galatians 2:20 (MSG)

Don't get me wrong, we *should* be enthusiastic about living in obedience to our Savior's will, but not without understanding some basic things about that relationship:

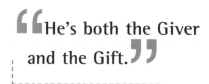

"He's both the Giver and the Gift."

- Our heavenly Father chose us as his own, adopting us into his family.
- He gifts us with his grace (his undeserved love), our motivator to follow the Savior.
- God promises we'll achieve true obedience the only way possible—through his grace and with his help.
- He gracefully extends his forgiveness through Christ to motivate us to continue to live for him even when we fail (and we will).

The common thread is that everything begins and ends with the Lord. He's both the Giver and the Gift. His gospel of love, help, and forgiveness motivates us to strive for obedience. Letting our egos take over and convince us we can impress God like we impress others just won't cut it. There's not enough good we can do to impress him in order to win over his favor. James 2:10 thumps us on the head every time: "For whoever keeps the whole law and yet stumbles at just one point is guilty of breaking all of it."

>>PIOUS IMPRESSIONS DON'T IMPRESS OUR IMPRESSIVELY GRACIOUS SAVIOR.

CTU doesn't allow any deviation from procedure. Neither does God. He demands 100 percent perfection—100 percent of the time.

Why do you demand the impossible, Lord? 100 percent? There's no way. How can our small successes impress our Savior with that kind of standard?

That's the point. We can't impress God. Pious impressions don't impress our impressively gracious Savior. We need his perfect life to cover our imperfect ones.

Why not gaze intently into Christ's mirrored heart of grace instead of our own rearview mirror of failures? When Jack Bauer looks in the rearview mirror of his day, he can't miss the human roadkill he left lying on the my-fault asphalt, the false pretenses buzzing around the roadkill like flies, the power struggles littering the pavement,

> **"Why not gaze intently into Christ's mirrored heart of grace, instead of our own rearview mirror of failures?"**

the failed relationships in tow, the vehicle of legalism riding his tail attempting to overtake him, and a stream of distrust flowing in the ruts made by the tire tracks of his intense life.

You know that little tab on the bottom of rearview mirrors that gives the driver the option of switching the view from night driving to light driving? The sin-producing junk we see in the rearview mirror is meant for driving in the dark. We hear legalism laying on its obnoxious horn, trying to get our attention. We see our failures flung all over the road.

Thankfully, Christ lives in us. We wisely let him take the wheel, and he flips the mirror's view-tab. The view changes drastically. We find our eyes looking forward, fixed on our Savior's mirrored heart of grace. Ahead of us lies a spotless one-way road—devoid of legalistic signs—filled with motivational

> **"If we're in love with the law, we're in an unhealthy relationship."**

billboards covered with both God's law and gospel, mapping the anything-but-routine route that runs through and to his grace-land. We're no longer driven to impress God; rather we're living with his perfect impression permanently embedded on our faith.

> The life you see me living is not "mine,"
> but it is lived by faith in the Son of God,
> who loved me and gave himself for me.
> I am not going to go back on that.
> —The apostle Paul, Galatians 2:20–21 (MSG)

"He Lived for the Law." That headline marked the death of Supreme Court Chief Justice William Rehnquist and obviously refers to constitutional law. As Christ followers how would we like those words, referring to God's law, on our tombstones?

Lots of people have a love affair with God's law. Some complain that I preach too much gospel. "Come on, Pastor, let us have it! We need the law to motivate us. Sure, you talk about our sins, but we *need* some good ol' fire and brimstone. You speak of forgiveness and grace. Throw the commandments in our faces! Scare the *hell* out of us, so we can make it into *heaven!*"

> **❝We've got to decide if we want to be motivated by fear or unconditional love.❞**

Here's the thing. Sure, the law can easily motivate us to keep on the straight and narrow. Legalism can motivate the *hell* out of us, but it's *not* the path to *heaven.* If we're in love with the law, we're in an unhealthy relationship.

I'm pretty confident our motivation to love grows stronger when someone says to us, "I love you unconditionally" instead of "You better love me ... *or else!*" Either statement can motivate us, right? We've got to decide if we want to be motivated by fear or unconditional love.

Let me set something straight. We need God's law. Without it, why would we need the freeing gospel? Rightfully, the law shows us our sins. We need to know and admit our sinfulness. But we also desperately need to know there is hope *beyond* our sins. Jesus Christ gifts us with his freeing forgiveness. We don't have to (can't, in fact) save ourselves from sin's deadly quicksand. Jesus came to do that for us.

> Is it not clear to you that to go back to that old rule-keeping, peer-pleasing religion would be an abandonment of everything personal and free in my relationship with God? *I refuse to do that, to repudiate God's grace.*
>
> —The apostle Paul, Galatians 2:21 (MSG)

Legalism flowed through the veins of the Pharisees during Jesus' life. They proudly focused on their 613 laws, as well as their perfection in keeping them. They looked down on the so-called "sinners." They tailed Jesus, hoping to catch him breaking the law. They hid around corners with their legalistic guns prepared to shoot their bullets—claims of heresy—into the Rabbi. They should have embroidered CTU (Counter Trust Unit) on their ornate headpieces.

They even stalked Jesus among stalks of grain (see Mark 2:23–28). Remember? Jesus and his disciples walked through a grain field. As they walked, the disciples picked some heads of the grain. And suddenly there was with the disciples (and Jesus) a multitude of legalistic Pharisees, raising questions and saying, "Glory to God in the highest, while on earth, these disciples are working on the Sabbath … the day of rest." Okay, that's not an exact quote, but the Pharisees lived so entrenched in the law that their hearts were hardened to anything else.

It's easy to pick on the bigger-than-life Pharisees. But I've got to confess, I need a good slap upside my faith with the reality of my pharisaic ways. I've looked down on others. I've trailed Jesus looking for loopholes in his Word. My pride shows when I do something I think would please and appease God. I silk-screened "CTU—Christ's Trusted Upper-crust" on my T-shirt. I've nearly stalked Jesus just to impress others.

That's my confession. Here's my prayer … *Lord Jesus, you've set me free from the law to live as a child of the Light, covered with your rays of grace. I don't want to go back to my old pharisaic ways. Why would I want to abandon the freedom you've won for me through your sacrificial death and your life-giving resurrection? I don't want to reject your grace—your undeserved love. Forgive me, Savior. Help me, Savior, to walk with you through grain fields, sports fields, dried-up fields, or even battlefields—wherever you want to take me and use me. I gracefully pray this in your freeing name. Amen.*

> If a living relationship with God could come by rule-
> keeping, then Christ died unnecessarily.
>   —The apostle Paul, Galatians 2:21 (MSG)

Legalism versus a forgiven life of joy and peace. Captivity versus reinstatement. That's the heart of the matter. According to Jesus, out of *our* hearts come evil thoughts, murder, adultery, sexual immorality, theft, false testimony, slander (Matt. 15:19). But out of *his* heart come full forgiveness, eternal hope, renewed joy, daily peace, new beginnings, amazing grace, and true freedom.

That's the heart of the matter.

That's *his* heart ... and all that matters.

Compassion Makes for a Great Passion

When he [Jesus] saw the crowds,
he had compassion on them,
because they were harassed and
helpless, like sheep without a
shepherd.
—Matthew 9:36

*The LORD is gracious and
righteous;
our God is full of
compassion.*

—Psalm 116:5

>>David Palmer: It just doesn't stop.

>>Jack: I'm sorry this is happening to you, sir.

>>David Palmer: You've been detained, your family's been
kidnapped, and you're concerned about *me?*

—Conversation in the CTU conference room

>>WITH TIME RUNNING OUT, THE
FORMER-STANDOUT-HOOPS-STAR-
TURNED-PRESIDENTIAL-CANDIDATE
CONFIDENTLY PUTS UP A SHOT
AGAINST THE CTU TEAM BY
DEMANDING TO SEE JACK BAUER.

His 6'4" frame and his intimidating résumé cause the team to stand out of respect. His demeanor demands admiration. His former John Wooden Player of the Year Award causes CTU team members to feel like freshmen walk-ons in front of a nationally acclaimed star. Palmer lays out his game plan. With time running out, the former-standout-hoops-star-turned-presidential-candidate confidently puts up a shot against the CTU team by demanding to see Jack Bauer.

Tony escorts Jack to the room. Rounding the corner, Jack stops in his tracks, both shocked and surprised. "Senator Palmer." The words meld into a paradoxical combination acknowledgment and disbelieving question.

"Sit!" Palmer harshly commands Bauer, like a head coach about to discipline his star player. Without contesting the authoritative figure, Jack sits, not about to question who's in charge. Wasting neither time nor words, Palmer verbally attacks, "I know *why* you want me dead, Mr. Bauer!" Without skipping a beat, Palmer continues with a three-syllable explanation, "Kosovo."

Bewildered, Jack softly responds, "Kosovo?"

"I know you hold me personally responsible for the men you lost there," Palmer states confidently, yet in a calmer tone. "Two years ago today."

"You know about Operation Nightfall?"

"I authorized the mission," the Senator informs a stunned Jack Bauer.

"I know you took out Victor Drazen and his inner circle. And I know you lost six men in the process." Palmer figures Jack is playing the game of revenge. Angered at the accusation, Jack stands and stridently sets the story straight with details of his actions and the kidnapping of his own family.

The tension in the room slowly defuses. Palmer realizes Jack's not on the opposing team. The two need each other and, realizing that, they begin to collaborate. Facts are shared and answers sought via CTU's vast array of technology.

>>You're concerned about *me?*

Within minutes, the two men's demeanors transform from livid to compassionate. Heart softened, Jack respectfully says, "I'm sorry this is happening to you, sir."

Taken aback, the Senator responds, "You've been detained, your family's been kidnapped, and you're concerned about *me?*"

Operation Nightfall II. This time the setting wasn't Kosovo, but St. Louis. Out of the darkness of a November night a young lady walked into the church where, at the time, I served as pastor. Oblivious to the fact that the Holy Spirit held her hand and led her here, I readily welcomed her in, along with her unseen companion. Seeing the open door and simple reception, her insecure eyes spoke for her, saying, *You're concerned about me?*

It became immediately obvious she really wanted and needed to talk to a Savior. That title certainly isn't on my résumé. I would simply take the role of liaison. As night fell that evening, the Spirit infiltrated this young lady's heart and my office, while her heart sang the blues. She began to open up.

The harsh melody of her life story grew to a crescendo of haunting tales as tears drenched the composition.

>>Why would God be concerned with me?

In the background one could hear her guilt drone on like a monotonous bass note. It was a dull, monotonous tone that sang—droned—from her soul.

>>Why would God be concerned with me?

She had sinned, and her joy was sapped by the guilt of her sin.

>>Why would God be concerned with me? Why would God have compassion on me?

>>SHE FINISHED HER CONFESSION AND STORY. BUT *HE* CONFESSED THAT HE WASN'T FINISHED WITH HER.

The sins were too vast and undoubtedly unforgivable ... or so she thought. She cried. She confessed. She shared her story. And then ... she finished, although her heart and soul yearned for peace, as the piece titled, "Why would God be concerned with me?" played on in her mind.

She finished her confession and story. But *he* confessed that he wasn't finished with her. Her Savior wasn't finished, because his aria, "It is finished," reverberated throughout a darkened arena one Friday afternoon.

> **"Overwhelmed, she truly realized she had a Savior who had a passion for compassion."**

Why would God be concerned with me? Jesus Christ wasn't finished. He longed to restore a joyful refrain of his salvation to her life.

>>Why would God be concerned with me?

Humbled, I realized the time had come for my ministry of serving as a compassionate liaison to pick up where the penitent left off. What an honor to introduce her to her compassionate, forgiving Savior-God. Contrary to her belief, he had a deep and loving concern for her. Without moving from our seats, I verbally took her on a trip to a hillside outside of Jerusalem called Golgotha—which means "The Place of the Skull." The only music most people heard at this place was the ever-unpopular funeral dirge ... played over and over again.

The Holy Spirit wanted to tune her ears to hear his love song of *life,* which Jesus would sing as part of a trio known as Father, Son, and Holy Spirit. The title of the tune he sang so gracefully? "Unforgettable Forgiveness." I played out the Savior's life song for her, with the accompaniment of the Holy Spirit.

Together we came face-to-face with the Living God facing death on the cross. There we prayed.

We praised his name. Repentant, we confessed our sins. Humbled, we begged for forgiveness. Confidently, by faith, we approached his throne of grace to receive tender mercy and find undeserved love to help us in our time of desperate need. Passionately, we prayed for a new beginning. Trustingly, we said, "Amen."

Overwhelmed, she realized she had a Savior who had a passion for compassion. She came to the realization that God *was* concerned about her. He was concerned about her sins. He was concerned about her guilt. He was concerned that she didn't believe he would forgive her ... until now.

As I wiped the tears from my eyes and began to sit back in my chair, I found out she wasn't finished. Why? Because Jesus once said, "It is finished!" I found out she wasn't finished praying. Her entire being prayed in praise of God's compassionate forgiveness and in gratitude for her new life.

> **"Slipping her hat back on, she again ran out into the darkness—while living in the light.""**

Jesus' heart went out to her, and she had to respond. She pulled the stocking cap off her head, clutching it near her heart. She fell to her knees on the office floor, still sobbing. But now her tears flowed from a grateful heart, joyfully overwhelmed by Christ's compassion. From the floor she looked up at me with a smile behind her waterfall of tears and asked, "I'm really forgiven, aren't I? He really loves me, doesn't he?"

With my own crescendo of joy I shouted, "Yes.... Yes! ... YES!"

This stranger ran back into the darkness—while living in the light—crying out, "I'm forgiven! He really forgave me!"

Awestruck in the presence of our compassionate, forgiving, miraculous Savior, I sat back in my chair and didn't have time to take it all in before she came bounding back in. She pulled the stocking cap off her head, again clutching it near her heart. She had one more thing to say ... "Thank you." Slipping her hat back on, she again ran out into the darkness—while living in the light. Operation Nightfall II was a divine success with only one loss accounted for in the process—a young lady lost herself in the compassionate heart of her Savior.

>>I LOVE THAT THE WORD *PASSION*
LIVES INSIDE COM*PASSION*.

I never saw her again, although I trust I will someday ... in heaven. Our only encounter was that night when God transformed my office into his workshop, also known as his throne room of grace. There, with two pieces of wood and three nails, he rebuilt a life ... make that two lives!

Compassion. It's one of my favorite words (since *chocolate chips* is two words). But more than the word, I love the act of compassion. I love that the word *passion* lives inside com*passion*. And to an even greater extent, I love to witness people living with a passion for compassion.

I'm not talking about them just feeling sorry for someone. It's much more than that. Jesus showed us that his passion beat in sync with his heart of compassion for all people, all nations, all races, all times.

The word *compassion* means your heart goes out to someone. That's what happened when Jesus encountered ...

- the grieving woman from Nain (Luke 7:11–17)
- a harassed and helpless crowd (Matt. 9:36)
- a crowd filled with sick people in need of healing (Matt. 14:14)
- followers who were hungry and exhausted (Matt. 15:32)
- blind men begging for sight (Matt. 20:30–34)
- a leper praying for healing (Mark 1:40–42)
- a world of sinners in need of a Savior (Rom. 5:8)
- ... to name a few.

Jesus' ministry of compassion touched those in his presence—the blind, the sick, the needy crowds, the hungry, the lame, the grieving. Those same needs for compassion live on in our presence today. He didn't heal every leper for all time. He didn't heal every blind person in sight. He didn't heal every deaf person you've ever heard of. Jesus' ministry of compassion touched those in his presence.

> **"His passion beat in sync with his heart of compassion for all people, all nations, all races, at all times."**

Today, Christ calls *us* to serve as his body on earth, to live with a passion for compassion. He calls us to serve as liaisons between our heavenly Father's compassionate ways and the world of hurting people—those who believe in Jesus as their Savior as well as those who wallow in unbelief.

A Christlike compassion comes to life in a million different ways. Situations differ, as do people. Jack Bauer's act of compassion in Season One: Episode 15 surfaces as a simple kind word to a frustrated presidential candidate. Heart softened, Jack respectfully tells Senator Palmer, "I'm sorry this is happening to you, sir."

Taken aback, the Senator responds, "You've been detained, your family's been kidnapped, and you're concerned about *me?*"

Eight words. That's all. Jack took the time to say eight words of compassion and a life was touched. Sometimes compassion is so simple, other times so complex.

Blessed with a passion for compassion, we may find ourselves ...

- giving a hug without needing to share one word
- in the middle of someone else's problems
- sharing our own messy shortcomings, to help others
- cleaning the sick or dying

- making sacrifices of time, money, or energy for the sake of others
- exhausted, but blessed
- covered with sweat and dirt from digging in to help
- putting the needs and wants of others before our own
- giving our lives
- ... or a million things in between.

So many acts of compassion go unnoticed and untold ... and rightly so. But when we are privy to those acts, they serve as great examples and sources of encouragement as the Lord leads us to others in need of Christ-driven compassion.

Jesus had a ministry of compassion for those who were in his presence. Who has he placed in your presence today? Yes, Jesus had a ministry of compassion for those in his presence. The miraculous fact of that truth is that *we* are in his presence now. His immutable promise tells us he will never leave us or forsake us—we'll *always* be in his presence.

Long ago, when he looked death in the face while on the cross, we were on his mind and in his compassionate heart. Still today, his heart goes out to us every moment of every day, any time we need him.

So many acts of compassion go unseen, yet doesn't it seem that as a people we're straying farther and farther away from our calling to "clothe [ourselves] with compassion" (Col. 3:12–14)? Instead, we clothe ourselves in restraining self-centeredness, so it's hard for our hearts to reach out to others. Our life song plays out of tune with Christ's compassionate song of life and forgiveness.

That's when heaven's divine trio of life takes us back to that hillside outside Jerusalem called Golgotha and its ever-unpopular funeral dirge. Repentant, we hear a different tune. It's a song of life! At the cross and empty tomb we find the answer to the refrain *Why would God be concerned with me?*

Responding to his answer, we ask, in Senator Palmer style, "Jesus, you've been abandoned by friends, detained by enemies, accused of a crime you didn't commit, abused verbally and physically, yet you're concerned about *me?*"

On perfect cue, Jesus, all of heaven, and all of God's people respond with a booming crescendo of joy and truth ... "Yes.... Yes! ... YES!"

In the middle of the day, in the middle of the darkness, in the middle of the longest day of his life, Jesus leaves us this example of his passion for compassion when he speaks from the cross ...

"Compassion sings a song of life at the door of death."

> Father, forgive them for they know not what they do.
> You will be with me in paradise.
> Here is your son.
> Here is your mother.
> It is finished.

Compassion sings a song of life at the door of death. The Singer dies. His song lives on. But a trio of days tells a world in need of compassion that the final measure wasn't final after all.

The Singer lives on ... and so does his song. It's an unfinished symphony of compassion and love, of forgiveness and life, of grace and peace. It's a song he sings to us—his ministry of compassion plays on through the ages for those in his presence. It's a song he wants us to learn by heart, in order that our hearts can go out to others.

>>Why would God be concerned with me?

Because he wrote you a song titled "Grace" with a melody line of compassion.

Chinks in the Link Have Different Meanings

Just then someone, without aiming, shot an arrow randomly into the crowd and hit the king of Israel in the chink of his armor. The king told his charioteer, "Turn back! Get me out of here— I'm wounded."
—1 Kings 22:34 (MSG)

>>It's real ... which is more than I can say for him.
—Elizabeth Nash, a Palmer staffer, referring to a diamond bracelet and its giver, Alexis Drazen, after she learns his true identity

God's love is meteoric, his loyalty astronomic,

His purpose titanic, his verdicts oceanic.

Yet in his largeness nothing gets lost;

Not a man, not a mouse, slips through the cracks.

—Psalm 36:5–6 (MSG)

Not even the Secret Service knows of the secret affair. She's seeking overt attention, gifts, and romance. He's seeking covert information, conspiracies, and itineraries. She craves *under cover* play. He craves undercover ploys. She's looking. He has the look.

>>Lust is blind.

She's not unassuming. He's assuming nothing. She uses her charm. He simply uses her. A staffer, she makes plans for the Senator. A terrorist, he plans to kill the Senator.

>>Lust is blind.

Elizabeth Nash knows little about Alexis Drazen. Little does Elizabeth Nash know she's a chink in the link to Senator Palmer. And little does Miss Nash know ...

>>Lust is blind ... and sometimes deadly.

> **"They found the chink in the defensive link. His name was Tim."**

My mom didn't want me to play football in high school. Finally, I talked her into it my senior year. I went to a small school where everyone made the team, so I didn't have to worry about getting cut. The coach even tried to comfort my mom by telling her he'd play me at the defensive cornerback position so the chances of my getting hurt weren't so great. She bought it, and I suited up.

During the first quarter of the first game, I made sure the receivers never touched the ball. Okay, okay, the truth is that their quarterback didn't throw any passes to the receivers, but that's beside the point.

>> WHAT'S YOUR WEAK SPOT? WE ALL HAVE THEM. HALF THE TIME, MY ACTIONS ACT LIKE A NEON SIGN FLASHING *WEAK SPOT! OPEN FOR BUSINESS! EASY ACCESS!*

In the second quarter, the other team lined up thirty yards from the end zone. The quarterback dropped back to pass and let it fly to the receiver I covered. Well, I was *supposed* to cover him. Wait a minute, where was the receiver? Oh great, he waited for the throw about ten yards downfield. The ball floated into his arms, he ran for a touchdown; I looked slow, inexperienced, and foolish. The other team's coach and quarterback weren't foolish, though. They knew a weak link when they saw it. The other team ended up scoring three more touchdowns on my side of the field. They found the chink in the defensive link. His name was Tim.

The story gets better, though. I wasn't going to live with the tag "Weak Link." I showed them my tough side. The play still plays fresh in my mind. The receiver jumped up to catch the ball, and just as it hit his hands I tackled him, ramming my body into his back, causing him to drop the ball. He lay there for a minute, obviously hurting a bit. I got back on my feet and leaned over him as he lay on the ground. Waiting for my manly football testosterone to kick in, I got right down in his face and said, "I'm sorry!" I kid you not. I told him I was sorry! The coach called me out of the game and said, "Wesemann, that was a good hit but you never, ever tell the opposing player you're sorry!"

Have you ever felt like the weak spot on the Family Team, the Work Team, the Church Team, or the Friendship Team? Hey, I spilled it, now it's your turn! What's your weak spot? We all have them. Half the time, my actions act like a neon sign flashing *Weak Spot! Open for Business! Easy Access!*

I realize I'm not the only one with a neon sign. One flashed on and off in *24: Season One:* Episode 16. In their revenge game with Senator Palmer and Jack Bauer, the Drazens found a weak spot. It was located in Elizabeth's heart. Just follow her flashing neon sign. Living in hotels and out of a suitcase, a political staffer can easily open the door to loneliness. Talking, eating, drinking, sleeping, breathing politics got old in a hurry. And the Drazen clan found a remedy for that.

> **"It's amazing how easily sin weakens the link with our Savior."**

They carefully scouted out a beautiful, young, lonely, single lady as their target and worked weeks ahead of the game to set their planned remedy and subterfuge into motion. Before the Senator and his team arrived in California for the primaries, Alexis Drazen seduced Elizabeth in order to infiltrate the team's inner circle. Little did he know that when Elizabeth uncovered his plan, the deadly game would turn 180 degrees. The ball landed in Elizabeth's deadly court, and you know what they say about a woman scorned. With a stab to his chest, Elizabeth took Alexis Drazen out of the assassination game and put him on the seriously disabled list.

We all have life-game stories of either being the weak spot or infiltrating the chink in someone else's link. Our own chinks leave a gaping hole in our armor. Which chinks, you ask?

>>LIFE IS ALL ABOUT OUR RELATIONSHIP WITH *THE* KING, ISN'T IT?

- Lusting for money
- Demoting others for the promotion
- Stealing for the thrill
- Gossiping for revenge
- Gambling out of greed
- Seducing for the risk
- Lying for fun
- Drinking to forget
- Overeating to mask pain
- Abusing for control
- Worrying for fear
- Plotting in secret

It's amazing how easily sin weakens the link with our Savior.

If you page through the books of 1 and 2 Kings or the summary books of 1 and 2 Chronicles, you'll find the names of generations' worth of Israelite and Judean kings. Each king's service before the King of Kings is usually summed up in these few or similar words:

> (name of king) did what was right in the eyes of the Lord,
>
> or
>
> (name of king) did evil in the eyes of the Lord.

Life is all about our relationship with *the* King, isn't it?

King Ahab's summary is longer than most. "Ahab son of Omri did more evil in the eyes of the LORD than any of those before him" (1 Kings 16:30). But should we give him a break and say that poor Ahab didn't have much hope since the Bible says the same thing about his father, King Omri? "But Omri did evil in the eyes of the LORD and sinned more than all those before him" (1 Kings 16:25). I guess it just runs in the family. One generation is worse than the last. Ahab and his father, Omri, were chinks in the link of kings who followed the will and ways of the Lord. The strong link between heaven's King and earth's kings had its share of weak and broken areas. Just page through those books of the Bible, and check out both the strong and the weak links.

> **❝Ahab called an emergency meeting of Prophets' Local Union #XXIV—about four hundred showed up.❞**

Not only did King Ahab create a weak spot in the kingly genealogy of Israel and Judah, but he also had a chink in his armor. *Literally,* he had a chink in his armor (see 1 Kings 22:29–37). Here's how the end of his life story played out …

For a time when Ahab served as king of Israel, Jehoshaphat served as king of Judah. Now Jehoshaphat "did what was right in the eyes of the Lord." (For the sake of brevity, let's shorten his name to *J-phat,* even if he didn't win a Grammy for Best Southern Rapper of 870 BC)

Anyway, Ahab and J-phat got together, and the evil king enticed J-phat to go with him into battle against Ramoth Gilead, in Aram, by telling him that the region belonged rightly to the northern and southern kingdoms. J-phat agreed, but only if they'd first seek the counsel of the Lord.

Ahab called an emergency meeting of Prophets' Local Union #XXIV—about four hundred showed up. By unanimous vote they gave the thumbs-up to resolution CLXXI—Wherefore, the kings of Israel and Judah seek counsel regarding the proposed battle to overtake Ramoth

Gilead, be it resolved that the aforementioned kings should pursue this battle immediately.

Good King J-phat wasn't convinced. He sought advice from one more of God's prophets, Micaiah, who had been blackballed by Ahab because he only spoke negatively against the evil king. Micaiah agreed with the vote of the other prophets. "Go! Be victorious!" But he added one other thing—kind of a chink in their plans. He said, "Ahab's going to, let's see, how should I put this? Ahab—you gonna die!"

Ahab lusted for victory, so he just laughed it off and made battle plans.

>>Ahab! Lust is blind.

The opposing team, the Arameans, couldn't wait to get rid of Ahab, so they welcomed a battle. Ahab plotted to outsmart them by smartly, he thought, setting up J-phat as a decoy. "I will enter the battle in disguise, but you wear your royal robes," Ahab instructed him (1 Kings 22:30). Heading to battle at Ramoth Gilead, the king of Aram told his warriors not to fight anyone except King Ahab, since everyone knew he lusted after greatness.

>>Ahab! Lust is blind.

The Arameans saw a king with royal garb and figured it was Ahab. Of course, it was J-phat, because that weasel Ahab disguised himself, wearing a suit of armor. As they attacked, J-phat yelled at them, and they realized they had the wrong guy; so they cut the attack short. They only wanted the wimpy king who lusted after self-preservation.

>>Ahab! Lust is blind.

Just then someone, without aiming, shot an arrow randomly into the crowd and hit the wicked King Ahab in the chink of his armor. The king told his charioteer, "Turn back! Get me out of here—I'm wounded" (1 Kings 22:34 MSG).

>>Ahab! Lust is blind ... and in this case, deadly.

A random arrow, huh? Hmm, you don't think God was behind it, do you?

> ❝My child, you did what is right in my eyes.❞

Well, Micaiah had it right. Ahab died. The chink in the link of God's appointed royalty died because of a chink in his own armor. What a creative God we have.

You know, I thought about God's summaries of the kings. They either did what was right in the eyes of the Lord or what was evil in his eyes. So how do the eyes of the Lord see us? If those were his two choices, we have to admit our link with the Lord has weak spots, and he could consider us evil. No doubt about it—we've done evil in his eyes. We deserve an arrow of death to pierce us through a chink in our personal armor.

But our God arranged a surprise ending. Our Savior took our armor filled with chinks and weak spots and exchanged it with the armor of God. His perfect armor covers our cheap, imperfect, death-magnetic armor. No flaws in this armor. God lined it with forgiveness. God polished it, not with Armor All, but with Hope-for-All.

Only because our God-given armor—which Christ, our Savior, bought for us—covers us will we hear the words, "My child, you did what is right in my eyes."

Heavenly Father, I thank and praise you that your love is not blind. Only you could have eyes that see me perfectly through the sinless life of Jesus, my Savior. Cover my weak spots—my entire life—with an armor free of chinks, gaps, or openings for Satan's arrows. Your love overwhelms and protects me, Lord. Amen.

Mirrors Don't Tell the Whole Story

We don't yet see things clearly. We're squinting in a fog, peering through a mist. But it won't be long before the weather clears and the sun shines bright! We'll see it all then, see it all as clearly as God sees us, knowing him directly just as he knows us!
—1 Corinthians 13:12 (MSG)

>>This place seems so familiar.
—Teri Bauer, looking around the restaurant

Those who hear [the Word] and don't act are like those who glance in the mirror, walk away, and two minutes later have no idea who they are, what they look like.

—James 1:23–24 (MSG)

>>(*Silence*)
—Teri Bauer studies herself in a mirror after suffering memory loss

Staggering, Kim reaches the top of the ravine's steep side, having survived the explosion that followed the car's plummeting crash from the shoulder of the road. Kim and Teri had fled the safe house, where CTU had sent them for protection, when they discovered someone had disclosed their whereabouts and they were again in danger. The demolished and burned-out car now smolders at the bottom of the cliff. Obviously shaken and confused, Kim repeatedly cries out for her mom. Her words rattle around the canyon and return, void of any response. Little does Kim know that questions are also rattling around her mother's mind, void of any explanations or answers. Amnesia tends to do that to a person.

>>Mom? Where are you, Mom? Mom!

Her words echo. Silence.

>>Where am I? (Teri questions, from a car somewhere down the nearby road.)

>>Where are you, Mom?

>>Why can't I remember?

>>Mom!

>>How'd I get here?

>>Mom!

>>And ... who am I? Wait! Pull over. That restaurant. I think I recognize it.

Teri and her Good Samaritan driver, Tanya, stroll into the restaurant hoping to find answers to Teri's meaningless questions.

On the wall hangs a friend of those looking for self-discovery. A mirror. What story will it tell Teri? Confused, she looks into the mirror hoping to discover the identity of the person looking back at her. Nothing. The mirror didn't tell Teri the story she needed to learn.

I'm spending time with my buddy today. I write; he hangs around my office. We're both happy with the arrangement. Buddy has an odd quirk regarding a mirror on the wall. He loves to look at himself in it and talk to himself. He spends half the day in front of that mirror. It's like he thinks the image in the mirror is another bird. Oh, I guess I forgot to mention my buddy, named "Buddy," is a parakeet. Parakeet people say birds think they have a friend in the cage. I don't have the heart to tell him he's actually alone!

Mirrors don't tell the whole story, for Buddy or any of us. When Teri Bauer looks in the restaurant mirror, she doesn't recognize the person she sees. Okay, granted, this time the writers pulled a story line straight out of the daytime soaps. *24*'s story lines are usually more sophisticated and creative than the temporary amnesia cliché but, nevertheless, the plot twist sets up a great faith truth discussion.

If you're like me (at least when I had a *real* job), you start the day in front of a full-length mirror (maybe coffee cup in hand). You're showered and dressed, ready to meet whatever the day throws at you. A quick mirror check is all that's left. You know the routine. We

- check out our hair and mess with it a little bit;
- turn our faces from side to side, hoping today's good side is *both* sides;

>>WHY *DO* WE LOOK INTO MIRRORS?

- move close to the mirror to check for blemishes;
- take a practice smile, reminding ourselves of the next step—making sure there's no food hangin' out on our teeth;
- step back and give ourselves the ol' once-over (sometimes the ol' twice- and thrice-over), making sure the day's wardrobe choice shouts "classy";
- quickly glance at our shoes (to see that they match, if nothing else);
- then think one of the following:
  - I've got to lose weight.
  - Wow! Am I good-looking or what?
  - Ugh, I look awful!
  - Not bad. Not bad.
  - I'm too skinny. (Well, someone might think that!)
  - Do these clothes make my butt look big?
  - Why do I even look in the mirror anymore?

Why *do* we look into mirrors? We're not the ones looking at us all day. Everyone else has to deal with our looks.

Well, motives vary from day to day and person to person. Some days we check to see whether it reflects the image we want. The good first impression issue often takes precedence. And, like all the up-and-coming people, we want to look successful. The artsy, free-spirited among us might choose to "express" ourselves in creative ways. Others want their reflections to shout, "Look at *me!*" After all, you can't get anywhere if people don't notice you, right? Or some want it to say, "I'm just like everybody else ... superficially, at least."

Those days we check the mirror hoping it'll reflect the story we want; other days we avoid looking, convinced it'll reflect a story we'd rather hide.

What story detail does each facet of that look reveal? The clothes? Facial expressions? Hair (or lack of it)? Skin color? Body shapes (whether pear, apple, or banana)? Jewelry or accessories? It's so easy to judge a look by its designer, isn't it?

>>CAN IMPRESSIVE "PROMOTION ATTIRE" CAMOUFLAGE DEPRESSED EMOTIONS?

Mirrors don't tell the whole story. Can ...

- a teeth-whitened smile mask the reality that we're gritting our teeth just to get by?
- a new, expanded wardrobe hide the fact we feel like the walls are closing in?
- a face-lift cover up the fact we need a faith lift?
- a haircut disguise our harried minds and bodies?
- impressive "promotion attire" camouflage depressed emotions?
- a pair of new shoes hide a dying soul?
- a $300 watch hide the fact we grow angrier hour by hour, minute by minute?
- a shamelessly buff body cover the shame of a secret sin?
- the reflection in the mirror hide the fear of rejection?

Mirrors don't tell the whole story. Following the car accident, Teri Bauer looks into the mirror and doesn't recognize the person she sees. If it were

"Kierkegaard leads us in prayer, 'And now, Lord, with your help I shall become myself.'"

possible for others to see into our not-so-pure thoughts, our struggles to do what's right, and our sinful inclinations to do what's not right, they likely wouldn't recognize the persons they see either.

Before we beat ourselves up too badly though, let's call on Søren Kierkegaard. The philosopher-theologian moves us away from the mirror that shows us our sin and the results of living in a sinful world. He escorts us to an open window, from which streams both the light of God's sun and God's Son. At the open window, Kierkegaard leads us in prayer, "And now, Lord, with your help I shall become myself."[1]

> **"Returning to the mirror we recognize the figure in the reflection with us. Jesus Christ."**

We suddenly realize we don't have to look in the mirror and accept what our eyes see and our minds know about the inside story. Through the power of the Holy Spirit who lives in us, a transformation stirs inside. Our eyes of faith begin to see more clearly. Returning to the mirror, we recognize the figure in the reflection with us. Jesus Christ.

He covers our lives—imperfections and all—bringing us into the perfect outline of his life. Graciously, he restores hope and banishes hopelessness. He trades his sure promises for our broken ones. He replaces fear with trust. He accepts us when others reject us. His love quiets our anxieties, our anger, and our feelings of abandonment. The Holy Spirit fans into flame the gift of faith within us.

Kierkegaard had it right. With the Lord's help—and *only* with his help and power-laced grace—we will become *ourselves*. Each of us will become the *self* God created us to be. It's right in front of us! The new

>> GRACIOUSLY, HE RESTORES HOPE AND BANISHES HOPELESSNESS.

"look" changes everything about us—our decisions, our concerns, our grief, our longings ... everything!

Remember Buddy? He has it right too. He looks in the mirror and sees another bird. He doesn't recognize himself. When Christ enters our lives, it's hard for us to recognize ourselves as changed—transformed and reformed. The apostle Paul writes this about Christ's transforming truth:

> Such confidence as this is ours through Christ before God. Not that we are competent in ourselves to claim anything for ourselves, but our competence comes from God.... Now the Lord is the Spirit, and where the Spirit of the Lord is, there is freedom. And we, who with unveiled faces all reflect the Lord's glory, are being transformed into his likeness with ever-increasing glory, which comes from the Lord, who is the Spirit. (2 Cor. 3:4–5, 17–18)

> **"God continually clarifies, refines, and defines that Christlike 'look' as we walk with him and live for him."**

We can't just stand there staring at this new creation in the mirror. This gift of changed lives works from the inside out—from the thoughts of our minds to the thrust of our actions. God continually clarifies, refines, and defines that Christlike "look" as we walk with him and live for him.

Jesus worked this transforming miracle within his disciples. Think about it. He called Matthew the tax collector to follow him. On the surface, this may not seem like a big deal, so we'll dig deeper. People saw Matthew as a social misfit. Devout Jews avoided tax collectors because they were usually dishonest. They almost had to be. Tax collectors didn't work for a salary, but were expected to make a profit by cheating those paying taxes.

Patriotic and nationalistic Jews hated them because they worked for the Roman government. Their hatred intensified if the collectors were also Jews, like Matthew, who were seen as betraying their own people by working for the *enemy*. So Jesus' selection of Matthew was a surprise to everybody, including probably Matthew.

> **"What amazing, miraculous transformations take place when Jesus walks into the reflection."**

Then Jesus called Simon the Zealot (not Simon Peter). The Zealots of that time were fanatical nationalists, determined to drive out the Romans by guerrilla tactics, ambushes, assassinations, terrorism, or whatever worked. We don't know if Simon was, or had been, a member of this order of Zealots, but it seems clear to me that Matthew and Simon the Zealot were at opposite ends of the political spectrum. Did they hate each other for their differences?

It would seem that Jesus' presence in their lives transformed their hearts. Matthew and Simon ate together, learned from Jesus together, traveled together, and, well, basically did most things together ... for at least three years!

What amazing, miraculous transformations take place when Jesus walks into the reflection.

As we began this chapter, we stepped in front of a full-length mirror. Remember the routine? Let's look again, through our eyes of faith. We're made clean by Christ's forgiveness and dressed in his love, ready to meet whatever the world throws at us. We look in the mirror before stepping out into the world. We

- check out the heir of heaven looking back (no one can mess with that promise);
- turn our faces toward Christ (who's always on our side);
- move closer to the mirror and to the Father (who sees only

perfection through Christ);

- take a look at our Savior-created smiles (no unforgivable sins hang on to *our* lives);

- step back and humbly give ourselves the ol' once-over (happy our lives shout, "Saved! Loved! Forgiven!" because Christ has clothed us with righteousness);

- look at our feet (fitted with readiness to share the gospel's peace);

- think all these thoughts:
  - ✓ Christ has removed the spiritual fat of my guilt and sin.
  - ✓ Wow! Does Christ look good on me or what?
  - ✓ Once I looked so bad; now I look divine.
  - ✓ Not bad. Not bad ... since Christ freed me to serve him.
  - ✓ I'm loving the opportunity to grow and grow in God's love.
  - ✓ I want to daily put on more of his Spirit-created gifts.
  - ✓ Amazingly, this heavenly wardrobe makes my heart so much bigger.
  - ✓ Why should I look back, through the mirror of the past, to the person I was before Christ came and made me a new creation by his love?

Most mirrors don't tell the whole story. Jesus is the story.

Remembering to Forget Creates Unforgettable Memories

For I will forgive their wickedness and will remember their sins no more.
—The Lord, Jeremiah 31:34

You got a problem with Jack, bury it.

—CTU District Director George Mason to Agent Hanlin, a sharp-shooter assigned to cover Jack as he walks into a crisis situation

>>*Who are you?*
>>*I'm a friend. A very good friend.*
>>*But I don't remember any of this.*
—Teri Bauer and Dr. Phil Parslow, former romantic interest, as Phil attempts to jump-start Teri's memory

The plaza serves as the perfect setting. Couples meet for lunch. The suits meet clients. Friends meet to visit at the outdoor tables, catching up on the news over an iced caramel macchiato. Strangers silently pass each other, rushing from point to point. In the middle of it all Jack Bauer waits to meet the man in the red hat—whoever he is.

Alexis Drazen set up the plaza meeting, but he's indisposed—something about meeting the welcoming committee at a surgery table in the ER. As Jack keeps the appointment with Palmer's would-be assassin in Drazen's place, he hopes the point man coming for the bogus bearer's bonds he carries won't discover he's not Drazen.

A sharpshooter scopes out the site, hiding among the ivy-laced walls overlooking the plaza.

>>The couples? Oblivious.

CTU agents mingle in the crowd, armed with not only hidden weapons but also expert training to spot potential threats anywhere, anytime.

"Jack Bauer paces the plaza, eyes darting across the ever-moving crowd, searching for a man he's never met."

>>The suits? Too caught up in business to notice.

Hidden earpieces and microphones in place, they patiently await word from Jack or Nina and secretly surround the perimeter, prepared to take action when or if called on.

>>The friends? Totally unaware.

Jack Bauer paces the plaza, eyes darting across the ever-moving crowd, searching for a man he's never met. He strains to remain focused as Agent Hanlin, CTU's sharpshooter, gets in Jack's head. Hanlin's voice clearly haunts Jack through the earpiece, and the scope zeros in on Jack, who roams through the crowd. It's tempting. Hanlin wants it so bad. His finger is eager to pull the trigger and fire a deadly, or at least a wounding, bullet into Jack's body. Hanlin despises being picked first to play on Jack's team. He not only hates having to work together on this case, he hates Jack. Hanlin can't let go of the past.

>>The sharpshooter. Positioned. Bitter. Unable to
forget.

It's been years since Jack turned in Hanlin's partner. Dirty agent, they charged him. Now he's in jail. And he just received word that his wife hung herself, leaving four children behind. Hanlin crams guilt into Jack's earpiece while making him a target of bitterness and a bullet. Bauer, Nina, and Mason plead with Hanlin over channel one. "You got a problem with Jack, bury it!" There's a job to accomplish.

Bauer paces. He scans the crowd. His eyes glance to the second level. "Hold up. I think I got him." A red baseball hat sits atop a man accessorized with a week-long growth of beard. The hat glides down the stairs with cautious confidence.

>>Jack? Primed. Edgy. Expectant.

While Jack meets an unknown contact in the plaza, miles away his wife searches desperately for her unknown past. Hearing about Teri's amnesia, Dr. Phil Parslow rushes to her side, hoping to jump-start her memory. Nothing. Nil. Nada. Her furrowed brow betrays her crashed memory drive. Will seeing her house cause a reboot? Nothing. The waiting game continues. The next move? Waiting for her husband and daughter ... whoever they are.

>>Teri Bauer? Confused. Distracted. Unable to
remember.

You might wonder about my interior decorating. The room's bright, bold blue, red, yellow, and purple. (I'm hoping it stimulates my creativity.) I've also surrounded myself with Cardinals baseball memorabilia, books, and a host of other fun stuff.

> **"It's a thing of beauty; a writer's best friend; an underappreciated joy in life ... I'm talking about the delete key."**

Because the cross is the focus of my writing and speaking ministry, Foolish Words (based on 1 Cor. 1:18), several unique crosses hang on the walls. On the wall behind my computer I painted, "Write for Him." Next to the words hangs a distinctive handmade metal crucifix. My favorite office accessory is a perfect reminder of those words and crosses. It's a little, nondescript black thing—approximately half an inch by half an inch in size—that came with my computer. It's a thing of beauty; a writer's best friend; an underappreciated joy in life. You guessed it; I'm talking about the delete key.

You see, my mind goes a mile a minute, but I can type only about three-quarters of a mile per minute. This predicament brings on a condition known as *Typo-fever*, and sometimes I done got it bad! Thank the Lord for the blessing of a delete key. The typo lives in fear of that tiny key; after all, it means permanent death to the misspeled—oops, make that *misspelled*—word.

> **"When it comes to deleting, computers have word-amnesia."**

Sometimes my editing demands drastic measures, and I reluctantly drag the mouse over the unwanted phrase, sentence, or paragraph, preparing whole chunks of verbiage for extinction.

The executioner curls his forefinger at just the right angle. In one swift moment, the finger moves downward through the air, and with gentle force depresses the delete key; the words disappear, soon to be forgotten. I tell you, it's a thing of beauty. And I'm not talking about sending it into the computer's recycle bin, where I can retrieve it at a later time. No, no, no. We're looking at complete extinction of those letters, words, and sentences.

If I want to put the deleted item back, I'll have to rely fully on my memory of what I originally wrote. When it comes to deleting, computers have word-amnesia.

I look forward to the day when someone creates a delete key for

>>A DELETE KEY FOR OUR WORDS AND ACTIONS WOULD CORRECT A LOT OF ARGUMENTS, HURT RELATIONSHIPS, AND PROBLEMS WE FACE.

words ... words I've spoken, sentences I've thought; entire paragraphs and documents that became actions. A delete key for our words and actions would correct a lot of arguments, hurt relationships, and problems we face. With deletion comes forgetfulness.

A new beginning follows deletion. We would have the opportunity to rephrase and rewrite our conversations. We'd have a chance to relive our actions, this time with much better responses. Hopefully those replacement words and actions would fall under the category of God-words and God-ways.

"Was I holding hands with a heretic?"

Years ago, as our family joined hands at the dinner table one evening, my daughter, Sarah, led us in prayer. "Thank you for this nice day and for school and for us being able to go outside and play. Thank you for this food. And thank you for dying on the cross and for saving our sins. Amen."

Wait a minute! I didn't want to say amen to the last line of *that* prayer! Was I holding hands with a heretic? We got it straightened out. Sarah made an honest mistake. She just forgot two words! Two little words. Two very important words that change the meaning of the sentence and prayer. My little heretic—I mean, daughter—meant to pray, "And thank you for dying on the cross and for saving *us from* our sins." Details, details! Unfortunately, for many people, the omission of that little detail doesn't seem to make that much difference.

Consider the two prayer options again: Thank you for dying on the cross and saving our sins. Or, thank you for dying on the cross and for saving *us from* our sins.

We gravitate to option two, and rightly so. But too often we live as though we've prayed the first one. The Devil tempts us to believe the first because he'd like to have us think he's powerful enough to make the charges stick.

Think about it. We easily thank God for Jesus' dying on the cross. That he died in our place, rose from the dead, and took our punishment is the crux of the Christian faith. Without that resurrection truth, faith doesn't make sense. Are you with me?

If we are in agreement, we have to ask ourselves a question. Why is

>>CTU AGENT HANLIN CAN'T *FORGET* THE PAST, WHILE TERI BAUER CAN'T *REMEMBER* THE PAST.

it so easy to *say* Jesus saved us from our sins while we *live* as though he saves our sins? I think it's safe to say we're all guilty of living in guilt because we believe God secretly has a list of our sins and can't wait to use it against us. Our life-song turns into a childish (not childlike) guilt-song, "Santa Claus Is Comin' to Town." Only we make the refrain, "Jesus Christ Is Savin' Our Sins."

Some of us may save stamps, coins, or baseball cards. But saving up sins ... sins that God has forgiven ... is not a good hobby. If we believe God hangs on to our sins, we'll hang on to them as well, even though we have repented of them and received God's forgiveness.

In Episode 18, CTU Agent Hanlin can't *forget* the past, while Teri Bauer can't *remember* the past. Hanlin is bitter, while Teri wants to get better. Hanlin wants payback, while Teri wants her memory back. They both have memory problems.

> **God has a case of permanent sin-amnesia.**

The *24* writers didn't avoid the amnesia tactic, and neither does God. When it comes to our sins, did you know that God has a case of permanent sin-amnesia? Too many people don't realize that fact. It's a life-changing truth for us. And if you have knowledge of it, don't assume everyone else does as well. Share this truth! Hand out this amazing news that has miraculous results.

Looking for more information on this condition of godly sin-amnesia? You won't find it written up in medical journals. But you can find it written up in the journals of Jeremiah, Isaiah, and David. Do the research. See for yourself.

> For I will forgive their wickedness and will remember their sins no more. (The Lord, Jeremiah 31:34)

> I, even I, am he who blots out your transgressions, for my own sake, and remembers your sins no more. (The Lord, Isaiah 43:25)

> For as high as the heavens are above the earth, so great is his love for those who fear him; as far as the east is from the west, so far has he removed our transgressions from us. (David, Psalm 103:11–12)

"We have a Savior who remembers to forget."

As you can see, our Lord has a serious case of sin-amnesia when it comes to his own. His condition comes without conditions. He promises his sin-amnesia is permanent; he will never hold our sins against us. "If you, O Lord, kept a record of sins, O Lord, who could stand?" (Ps. 130:3). He's created the ultimate delete key. God's delete key works faithfully, so we won't be deleted from his grace! We have a Savior who remembers to forget.

By the way, you should know that if you get close to him, you might catch his sin-amnesia. It's contagious.

Dull Doesn't Describe Our Lives

We'll sell you the whole seat,
but you'll only need the edge!

—Ad for a championship tractor pull

Everything's boring, utterly boring—
no one can find any meaning in it.
Boring to the eye, boring to the ear.
—Ecclesiastes 1:8 (MSG)

>>I gotta tell you, Jack, it
never gets dull with you!
—CTU District Director
George Mason

Less than one second. That's all it takes. A bullet streaks so fast, so silently that no one notices until it penetrates the torso of the man in the red hat. The jolt of the impact knocks him off his feet and sends him crashing through the plaza railing. His body and the concrete walkway one story below become one. One second he's known as the man in the red hat, and the next he's the dead man in the red hat.

>>I gotta tell you, Jack, it never gets dull with you!

> **"Correct me if I'm wrong, but what this day basically boils down to is a personal vendetta against you and Palmer by the family of Victor Drazen?"**
> —George Mason to Jack Bauer

Less than one minute earlier, things were different. Looking for a handoff of $50,000 in bearer bonds from Alexis Drazen, the unknown contact finds himself sitting across the table from Jack Bauer, the Drazen imperson-ator. Drazen is late, and likely soon to be the *late* Alexis Drazen. Before the unknown contact becomes suspicious of Jack and bolts, Bauer squeezes some vital information out of him. The assigned mission, including a planned shut-down of a specified power grid for five minutes, at exactly 7:20 p.m., takes him only a few words to detail.

>>I gotta tell you, Jack, it never gets dull with you!

Less than five minutes. That's how long it takes Jack to run with the new information. District Director Mason chauffeurs Jack in an official CTU car as they head down the road, unsure of what they'll find. During the ride, Jack fills in the blanks for Mason, who is oblivious to the last few hours' events. Mason shows he's a quick study, "Correct me if I'm wrong, but what this day basically boils down to is a personal vendetta against you and Palmer by the family of Victor Drazen?" Then comes the obvious:

>>I gotta tell you, Jack, it never gets dull with
you!

At the CTU offices, Nina and Tony gather data on the exact location of the power grid. GPS maps fly through the cyberworld, landing within Jack's palm-sized computer. Looking like Al playing with his futuristic gizmo on *Quantum Leap*, Jack sifts through satellite maps to establish the location of a mystery address within a designated wildlife sanctuary.

Jack moves through the wooded area like a hound dog picking up a scent. His nose sniffs out a locked power transformer in the middle of nowhere, while Mason follows, lacking a Bauer-like passion for this mission. Led by the GPS, the agents move into a nearby clearing, supposedly the precise location of the mysterious address.

>>WHAT MOVIE TITLE BEST DESCRIBES
YOUR LIFE AT THIS MOMENT?

The agents stand mystified as the orange sun sets. Breaking the silence of the wilderness, the distinctive whirling of an uninvited and unexpected helicopter rises dramatically over the horizon. The intensity rises as the copter encircles Bauer and Mason.

>>I gotta tell you, Jack, it never gets dull with you!

What movie title best describes your life *at this moment?*

- *Life Is Beautiful*
- *Rocky*
- *One Flew Over the Cuckoo's Nest*
- *Turning Point*
- *All Quiet on the Western Front*
- *Just Like Heaven*
- *As Good as It Gets*
- *The Road to Perdition*
- *Catch Me If You Can*
- *Rush*

I guess we can also throw out a television show—not the title, rather its premise:

- *Seinfeld*—the show about nothing

What if you picked one that described your life last week? last month? last year at this time? There's likely a lot of variance in your answers. I know my response would almost certainly change from week to week, often day to day. So many variables play a part in our answers.

What changes the atmosphere of your day? Office politics? Mood of a friend, spouse, or family? Size of your commission check? The weather? Love life? Day of the week? Physical condition? Work environment? Worship time? Traffic jams? The mail? Or the ever-popular bad hair day? So many variables, so little consistency. That's life! Dull doesn't describe our lives.

> **" So many variables, so little consistency. That's life! "**

CTU District Director George Mason says, "I gotta tell you, Jack, it never gets dull with you!" If you had to replace Jack's name with yours within the words of Mason, would the comment accurately describe your life?

>>I gotta tell you, _____, it never gets
dull with you!

> **" If today were a chapter in my life, I'd have to title it 'Untitled.' "**

Where, on a scale of 2–13 (just trying to add some zip from the dull 1–10 scale), does your life fall (2 is very dull and 13 is anything but dull)? Would others agree with your assessment? How do you think God would gauge your level? Are you, perhaps, a little lazier on those dull days?

Allow me to share a devotional piece I wrote years ago about a very dull, lazy day that God turned around.

UNTITLED (subtitle: TITLED)

If today were a chapter in my life, I'd have to title it "Untitled." It was my day off. My wife and children were out of town, and I didn't do anything!

As I laid my head on my pillow at the end of the day, I realized I was a good-for-nothing bum. The day seemed wasted. I didn't get one thing crossed off my "Honey-do" list. I ate leftovers, so there wasn't any cooking to do besides pushing a few microwave buttons. I took a nap (pushing those buttons can really wear a guy out). The TV worked overtime on my untitled day. I even used up all of the hot water in a skin-pruning shower. And then it was time for bed. Where had the day gone?

>> I NOTICED IT BECAUSE THERE WASN'T ROOM FOR ME TO SET DOWN MY TWINKIE AND GLASS OF FRUIT PUNCH (A PERFECT WAY TO CAP OFF AN UNTITLED DAY).

Have you ever had one of those days? Come on, admit it! Please! I can't stand the guilt if I am the only one! (Thank you for your honesty.)

You know, during my untitled day I was more than lazy. I was unfaithful to God. I was a bad steward of my time. I don't remember issuing one prayer (not even for a little zest). I didn't turn a page in my Bible. I don't know that I shared God's love with anyone. I made fun of an actor on a dumb television commercial. When the dog started barking, I barked back. What an ugly, useless day! Now I'm not promoting laziness. These untitled days are few and far between—thank goodness! But the Lord taught me something about his love for me as I lay me down to sleep that night.

As I went to bed on that untitled night, I noticed my Bible open on the nightstand. I noticed it because there wasn't room for me to set down my Twinkie and glass of fruit punch (a perfect way to cap off an untitled day). I had to move the open book to make room for my midnight snack. As I moved it, my eyes caught a glimpse of Isaiah 45:4: "For the sake of Jacob my servant, of Israel my chosen, I summon you by name and bestow on you a title of honor, though you do not acknowledge me."

Suddenly I lost my taste for a snack. I was on holy ground. God was speaking to me. For the sake of Jacob, God acknowledged King Cyrus, even though Cyrus didn't acknowledge God.

> **"We need to allow God to lead us into those times of rest."**

I looked down again. This time it seemed to read differently. "Tim, for the sake of Jesus, my Son, your Savior, I summoned you by name and bestowed on you a title of honor, even though you did not acknowledge me today."

I put the snack on the floor and returned the Bible to the nightstand. I turned off the TV and the light. I prayed.

"Forgive me, Father, for the sake of Jesus, your Son, my Savior, for my sins of laziness and unfaithfulness, and for my attempts to leave you out of this day you entrusted to my care. But thank you for your grace ... even when I fail to acknowledge you in my days."

What a day it turned out to be. This was a day that the Lord had made. God helped me rejoice and be glad in it.

God has called me by name to be his. I am God's child. What a title of honor! I think I'll subtitle this brief chapter in my life: "Titled!" That has a nice, true ring to it.

I can't wait to see what God titles tomorrow.

Let me quickly add an addendum to this story. I don't want anyone to feel guilty about taking time to relax and recharge. That's important and necessary. But we need to take God with us. Let me rephrase that. We need to allow God to lead us into those times of rest. That's his desire. Throughout his ministry, he left us examples of the importance of getting away, resting, and spending time with the Father. There's a difference between laziness and godly rest.

Mark 6:30–56 describes two times Jesus got away to rest and pray while being pulled in thirty-seven directions. The first time, the siesta plan was short-lived. The second time, it worked out for him.

It's an understatement to say Jesus desperately needed a time-out. Check out his day's or possibly two days' schedule as recorded in Mark 6.

- His trip home was anything but encouraging—his family and neighbors were embarrassed by his claims and presence (6:1–6).
- His public teaching schedule increased to full time (6:6).
- He prepared and sent his coworkers on a business trip—to be about the Father's business (6:6–13).
- He learned his relative was murdered and buried (6:14–29).
- He didn't have time to debrief his coworkers upon their return (6:30).
- His meal plans were scrapped—no time (6:31).
- He postponed his attempt to find some quiet, restful time (6:32–33).
- Without prep time, he threw together an outdoor "arena" for an overflow crowd expecting a speech (6:34–37).
- He prepared a meal for thousands of people (6:35–44).
- Following the group meeting, he sent his friends on a boat ride, hoping he could find some time alone to rest and pray (6:45–46).
- He spent time in a private prayer vigil in the mountains (6:46).
- He took a peaceful walk ... on the water (6:47–50)!
- He calmed his frantic friends (6:49–52).
- And soon the cycle started over again as he met with more crowds and healed their sick (6:53–56).

Whew! I'm worn out just reading about his busy day! Obviously, Jesus understands our anything-but-dull days. At the same time, he leaves us an example of the importance of stillness, solitude, prayer, time with the Father, and a Sabbath day of rest.

>>I gotta tell you, Jesus, it never gets dull
with you!

And he responds, "And also with you!"

The Lion Doesn't Sleep Tonight

Be self-controlled and alert. Your enemy the devil prowls around like a roaring lion looking for someone to devour.

—1 Peter 5:8

>>You know what, Jack, I take back what I said. It's getting dull.

—CTU District Director George Mason

>>You're not qualified to tell me the truth.

—Senator David Palmer to his wife, Sherry, who's been manipulative and self-serving, lying for political gain

But I trust in you, O Lord....
My times are in your hands;
deliver me from my enemies
and from those who pursue me.

—Psalm 31:14–15

The clock is ticking ...

Confident he'll untangle the thread of information and uncover the importance of 7:20, the exact time his enemies planned to have the power cut in this quadrangle, Jack checks his watch without losing a step. It's here. In the middle of nowhere. Something's here. Something important.

>>The clock is ticking ...

Jack sprays the flashlight's beam from side to side as he walks through a small ravine. It's here. Something's here. Something important.

>>The clock is ticking ...

Jack moves his head in rhythm with the beam of light until his eyes focus on a short wall with an opening on one end. He shakes off his "deer caught in the headlights" look, jumps a fence, and runs cautiously toward the unidentified discovery.

A passageway surrounded by concrete blocks leads into the earth. Jack's body language says, "It's here. It's *right* here." He steps into the stairwell without realizing eyes are watching him. Binoculars follow Jack's moves until he disappears into the earth.

>>The clock is ticking ...

An electronic shriek ricochets intensely off the walls as Jack steps into the underground corridor blocked by a concrete door. He's trapped. Powerful flashing lights cause Jack to cover his eyes, making it difficult to see the door slide open to reveal two guards in full service gear. Immediately, they shoot the trespasser time and time again with high-voltage stun guns. Jack's body pulsates violently with each hit, and he collapses like a wounded deer.

>>The clock is ticking ... but Jack's heart ticks

faster.

Outside the underground compound, Drazen and his camouflaged team of armed mercenaries wait impatiently for 7:20 to arrive, along with the helicopter carrying the prisoner they desperately want to free.

Coughing, gagging, and vomiting, Jack rudely awakens in an underground holding cell. Mark DeSalvo enters and tosses Jack's wallet at him. DeSalvo, a Department of Defense agent, has checked out Jack's identity and discovered they are on the same side. A dialogue ensues and plans are made as the minute hand closes in on twenty minutes after seven. Every second is valuable; every conversation important; every decision significant.

DeSalvo has little information to share except that at 7:20 a prisoner is being delivered by helicopter. The prisoner's identity is classified, top secret. The Department informed DeSalvo only that it moves him to a new location every few weeks.

Bauer, DeSalvo, and his small staff outfitted in full combat gear emerge from the prison that doesn't really exist to bring in a prisoner who doesn't seem to exist. Jack knows the power won't go out, having taken care of that detail earlier. Without the light failure, the mercenaries, still hiding on the perimeter, know they can't attack and free the prisoner.

Under the whirling blades of the helicopter,

DeSalvo's men hurry the prisoner into the underground prison. Once in lockdown, Jack can't believe he's looking into the eyes of a man he killed two years ago. Victor Drazen. The patriarch of the Drazen clan.

>>The clock is ticking ... while Jack's ticking
heart pauses in disbelief.

It started innocently enough and grew into a disaster of enormous proportions involving terrorists, mercenaries, and assassins. Jack had gathered a lot of information. The CTU experts even estimated the time of arrival—7:20 p.m. People responded to the situation differently. Jack stuck it out. Mason moved on. The results of the damage wouldn't be known for a while. The enormity of devastation could affect lives everywhere, since the life of a potential U.S. president sat in the balance.

❝Disasters start so innocently and end up leaving a trail of destruction behind.❞❞

Her birth began in the usual way as the water around her broke. Her personality was evident from her inception. The painful contractions somehow caused the tiny-muscled baby to twist and thrash abnormally. Her long, excruciating birth brought with it a dramatic reality—this was no ordinary birth or baby. They named her Katrina, a sweet, serene name meaning "pure." But names can be deceiving.

Soon, all eyes were on this precocious newborn, wondering how she would handle the path set out for her. Her tranquil name became a misnomer. As she grew, Katrina chose a tumultuous path. In fact, she matured into one of the worst serial killers in the United States. Wanted in at least three states for her deadly activity, Katrina left a trail of destruction along her path. A killer with a sweet name.

It starts innocently enough in our lives too. The day is filed under *U* for "uneventful." We might as well put our cars on autopilot—they know the routes we take. Unexpectedly, the warning siren goes off: "Keep a cool head! Stay alert! The Devil is poised to pounce, and would like nothing better than to catch us napping" (based on 1 Peter 5:8 MSG).

We flick the warning off in our ears, as if it were only a practice drill on the radio, and go about our mundane business. That's when hell's mercenary pounces into action. He begins with something innocent, so as not to draw attention to the temptation. Sometimes he disguises temptation as something that at least looks good. Maybe he even chooses a serene name to throw us off. Once he gets the ball rolling, he tries his best to keep it moving in the wrong direction, convincing us that the wrong direction is the right direction.

Disasters start so innocently and end up leaving a trail of destruction behind.

- The spring wind blows gently through open windows, causing the curtains to come to life. Hours later the wind has turned into a full-blown tornado breaking windows, trees, and hearts—causing terror to come to life.

- The get-together begins with a few friends sharing conversation and some drinks. Hours later the get-together turns into a full-blown party with no designated driver in sight. The BYOB bash leads to a DUI and a DOA.

> Be self-controlled and alert. Your enemy the devil prowls around like a roaring lion looking for someone to devour. (1 Peter 5:8)

- The campfire provides warmth, light, and memories, but

when the campers go home a miniscule spark lands on a dry leaf, quickly igniting and spreading. Before you know it, a wildfire rages, sparking fear, anxiety, and unwanted memories.

- The morsel of gossip provides laughter and stunned looks; but when the workers go home, the gossip spreads and sparks more conversations. Before you know it, a reputation is smoldering, sparking resentment, bitterness, and depression.

> **"We all know where the enemy regularly prowls in our neighborhoods, workplaces, and homes."**

Be self-controlled and alert. Your enemy the devil prowls around like a roaring lion looking for someone to devour. (1 Peter 5:8)

- The raindrops splash playfully on the porch, cleaning and cooling the air. But when the rain won't let up, riverbanks spill over, bringing a flood of emotions, causing panic to reign each morning and night.
- The two flirt playfully on the boss's porch, impressing and putting on airs. But when the flirting won't let up, passion spills over, bringing a flood of emotions and causing guilt to reign in the morning because of what happened at night.

Be self-controlled and alert. Your enemy the devil prowls around like a roaring lion looking for someone to devour. (1 Peter 5:8)

- San Andreas. New Madrid. Denali. Loma Prieta. Majestic, serene names, but their activity causes people to quake in terror. They have their faults—which can tear apart homes, businesses, and lives.

- Powerball. Keno. Mega Millions. Roulette. Powerful, enticing names, but the activity can cause addiction-driven people to quake with faulty expectations and can tear apart families, relationships, and lives.

Be self-controlled and alert. Your enemy the devil prowls around like a roaring lion looking for someone to devour. (1 Peter 5:8)

All these start so innocently but can end so disastrously.

We all know where the enemy regularly prowls in our neighborhoods, workplaces, and homes. I read a book that might help us. I can't find the author's name anywhere, but I think you'll like it. One book at a time is all you care to read? Believe me, it's only five chapters—a quick read.

The Five-Chapter Story

Chapter One

I was walking down the street, and I fell into this big hole. It wasn't my fault. It was dark and scary, and it took me a long time to get out.

Chapter Two

I was walking down the same street, and I fell into this big hole. It was still dark and scary; but it was familiar, so I knew how to get out quickly.

Chapter Three

I was walking down the street and saw this big hole. I chose to jump in and got out quickly.

Chapter Four

I was walking down the street and saw this big hole. I chose to walk around it.

Chapter Five
I walked down a different street.

The End. No ... the Beginning!

Interesting read, don't you think? I like that it ends with the beginning. That's the way all our daily life stories should end—with a new beginning. And that's what we find—a new beginning—when we walk down Grace Boulevard instead of Temptation Alley or Disaster Drive in the city of Living Hell.

In the middle of Grace Boulevard sits the Disaster Relief Shelter. It's usually packed, yet no one ever has to wait for service and help. Broken pieces of lives are everywhere. Emotional burn victims who played with fire find miraculous healing through a life-giving process of repentance and forgiveness. You never need an appointment to find help with disappointments—no matter if they're Bauer- and Drazen-sized debacles, Katrina-like induced calamities, or your everyday-sized difficulties.

The head of the shelter provides his own blood to transfuse every disaster victim who crosses the threshold. He provides nourishment with a recipe of mercy mixed with living water and served with the cup of thanksgiving. He also makes permanent shelters available for those who have lost their jobs, families, or minds in hellacious emotional storms.

Many at the shelter have parts of their lives torn apart after a devilish lion attacks with temptation out of nowhere, making an offer too good to resist. For those, the shelter's leader supplies an IV of forgiveness—not one that hangs on a hospital pole. No, this IV is hooked up directly into the heart of the owner of the shelter while he hangs from a cross.

The Disaster Relief Shelter looks ordinary enough from the outside. But when the doors open and you are welcomed inside ... ahhhhhh. You realize why it sits on *Grace* Boulevard.

You Didn't Get There by Yourself

I am the vine; you are the branches. If a man remains in me and I in him, he will bear much fruit; apart from me you can do nothing.
—Jesus, John 15:5

It looks like he may have gotten a boost in the late vote based on the roller coaster events of his day.

—TV news reporter announcing Senator Palmer's sweep of the primaries

>>I want to thank everyone in this room for their support. This is *our* victory.
—Senator David Palmer to his staff and supporters after sweeping the Super Tuesday presidential primaries

Bouquets of red, white, and blue balloons sprinkled generously throughout the suite shout, "Victory!" Champagne glasses rise and clink in celebratory fashion. Smiles radiate from every face. Laughter makes its rounds but subsides when the candidate calls for the floor. "This is *our* victory! This is our night!" Let the celebration begin! A year's worth of election-tension flies out the window—at least for twenty-four hours, after which it all starts up again. The road to the White House is paved with exhausting work and demands extraordinary energy.

>>Let's move the victor into the White House!

>>Let's move Victor out the back way!

Power's out! Victor Drazen must be moved. The scent of Victor's sons and their mercenaries isn't faint anymore. They're closing in. Jack, like a mouse in a maze, frantically calls for help from DeSalvo to get them out of the underground prison before it's too late. Not knowing the layout, Jack realizes he can't do this by himself. DeSalvo leads them toward th—

> **"He knows he didn't get there by himself."**

An explosion rocks the top-security prison, throwing Jack, DeSalvo, and his men against the wall. They stagger back to their feet, stunned. New plan! New direction! Turn around! This way. Through it all, Jack never loses sight of the prize possession—one handcuffed, yet deadly, Victor Drazen. He's the prize both sides want ... desperately.

The presidential candidate isn't just saying what his staffers want to hear—that's not his style. He means it. Senator David Palmer prefers honesty. He knows he didn't get there by himself. And he's going to give credit where credit is due. When the TV newscaster announces Palmer has swept every primary on Super Tuesday, the Senator stops and thanks his staffers and supporters. "This is *our* victory!" Palmer knows a lot of people helped carry him to victory.

Another man knows he needs people to carry him. Their response floors him. By himself, he doesn't have a leg to stand on—literally. He is paralyzed. So friends carry him to a spot where the foot traffic is heaviest. More people mean more money. More people, more chance for a morsel of food. His friends set him down to begin his business of begging, ask if he needs anything else, and go on about their own business. Traffic flow is usually good at this spot; he is glad to get here before others claim it. But traffic seems to be diverted today—to the house across the way.

> **"By the looks of the crowd ... you'd think the Roman circus had come to town."**

It must be big news. An overflow of people pour out the front door. Standing Room Only passes seem to be the hot ticket to this main event. It certainly piques our friend's curiosity, and frustrates him at the same time. He thinks about sending out invitations to a pity party. No one gives him the time of day, let alone a piece of day-old bread. By the looks of the crowd surrounding the house, you'd think the Roman circus had come to town.

Then he notices four men leaving the crowd. Maybe they don't like the show, or they are sick on a Big Top Kosher hot dog. He begins to make out their faces as they walk toward him—the four faithful friends who regularly give him a lift. Without explanation, each man takes hold of a wooden pole on his stretcher—two at his head, two at his feet. Walking in rhythm to avoid jostling their paralyzed friend too much, they hurry toward the house, with the name of Jesus on their lips.

>>THEY HURRY TOWARD THE HOUSE, WITH THE NAME OF JESUS ON THEIR LIPS.

Does the story ring a bell? Read it again in Mark 2:1–12. These four friends believe Jesus can heal all, but they can't reach him because of the crowd. Somehow though, their creativity, their compassion, and their faith prevailing, they manage to pull their companion, stretcher and all, to the roof of the house. Wouldn't we have loved to see how they got him there? Did one of them carry ropes and pulleys in his robe pocket, just in case? Do I smell a winner on Capernaum's Funniest Home Etchings? I mean no disrespect for the powerful miracle that unfolds next, but what an interesting work of love and determination sets the scene for it.

Once there, the four men first dig a hole in the thatchlike roof. (I guess the homeowner could file an insurance claim, denoting it literally an act of God, or at the least, an act *for* God!)

The scene then shifts inside, to Jesus. He's busy teaching, when suddenly straw and particles of mud drop on him from somewhere above. Plop! He shakes them out of his hair and flicks them off his shoulders as if they're dandruff. He spits a little piece of straw off his lips. Does he continue to teach, knowing what will happen next, or does he join the others, staring up, waiting for the roofers to stop? What a sight.

> **"Do I smell a winner on Capernaum's Funniest Home Etchings?"**

But it gets better. Observers look up to see, not a tiny hole in the roof, but rather one big enough to get a paralyzed man and his stretcher through! Sure enough, as those in the crowd squeeze even closer together to make room, the men lower their paralyzed friend to the feet of Jesus (who might still have a piece of straw stuck in his hair). Don't you think we should consider *their* actions the first miracle at this house?

The second, and most incredible, miracle happens next, when Jesus says, "Son, your sins are forgiven" (Mark 2:5). Too often I forget that, indeed, forgiveness is a miracle—and a far greater miracle than Jesus' physical healing of the man (which he also does). Think about that a minute. We marvel and marvel when someone is healed. How often do we marvel at the miracle of forgiveness? If matters of faith, like forgiveness, affect us for eternity while matters of health affect us for only this life, which are more important? Let's put things in perspective, shall we?

> **"Too often I forget that, indeed, forgiveness is a miracle—and a far greater miracle than Jesus' physical healing of the man."**

>> **IF MATTERS OF FAITH, LIKE FORGIVENESS, AFFECT US FOR ETERNITY WHILE MATTERS OF HEALTH AFFECT US FOR ONLY THIS LIFE, WHICH ARE MORE IMPORTANT?**

This buffetlike passage contains another interesting morsel. I don't recall Jesus responding in this manner other times, although he may have. Just after the men worked successfully to bring the man to his Savior, Jesus saw *their* faith and forgave the man's sins. The part-time roofers/part-time Acme stretcher-taxi drivers/full-time believers played a part in Jesus' gifting the man with forgiveness. We shouldn't assume the paralytic didn't have faith of his own, but the word used is definitely plural—"When Jesus saw *their* faith ..." (2:5).

>> IT WAS HIGH FIVES ALL AROUND THAT ROOF, I'LL BET, IF THEY'D BEEN INVENTED THEN.

Put yourself inside that house and look up at the hole in the roof. I love picturing four faces filling the void—their owners lying on their stomachs to get a bird's-eye view—witnessing firsthand the miracle of forgiveness *and* the miracle of healing. At Jesus' word the man picks up his mat and walks out in full view of everyone. It was high fives all around that roof, I'll bet, if they'd been invented then. High fives, not prideful, but in praise of Jesus' miracles and heavenly power. We're told the people praised God. Ahhh, another matter of faith. They had never seen anything like that before.

Oh, if we'd only remember and praise God for the life-giving power and grace of Jesus' presence in our lives. Where would we be without him?

We're like the proverbial turtle on top of a fence post. We know he didn't get there by himself. And neither did we.

The paralytic couldn't have come to Jesus by himself. People carried him to his Savior. Surely God placed friends in his life for a purpose. The man couldn't forgive his own sins. The man couldn't earn forgiveness for his sin-filled life, nor could he put life back in his limp legs. But Jesus could, and did.

Will you join me in a minute-long break (or take as long as you'd like or need)? Picture the paralytic's stretcher/mat and the four people who surrounded and carried him to Jesus. Which four people has God brought into your life to help carry you into the presence of Jesus? Who didn't let you down by letting you down on your stretcher in front of Jesus? Maybe you'll want to turn to Mark 2 and in the margins draw a little stretcher with four handles. There you can list the names of four of the people who have helped carry you to Jesus. What miracles did Jesus bring you as he said, "Take up your matters of faith and walk out of here, for-given"? Did the miracles fill your life with gratitude and praise?

> **"Who carried you into the presence of Jesus?"**

We won't get anywhere without our God. Without him, we are spiritually paralyzed.

We can't create faith within our lives or forgive all our sins or save ourselves or give ourselves the gift of heaven. Those are all God's mirac-ulous gifts. We can't even bring ourselves to get up and walk. That's God's miraculous gift again ... and again.

Senator Palmer realized the victory wouldn't now be his without his staff having given their all. Jack Bauer knew he couldn't have gotten out of that prison without help.

Where would we be without our God, without our Savior, without his Holy Spirit?

- We couldn't give Christ our all without first kneeling at his cross.
- We couldn't take up our cross without first observing Christ's example.
- We couldn't be an example without first seeing how Jesus served.
- We couldn't serve without first receiving God's love.
- We couldn't love without Christ first living in us.

- We couldn't live without first experiencing our Savior's grace.
- We couldn't offer grace without knowing of his sacrifice.
- We couldn't live sacrificially without first receiving his forgiveness.
- We couldn't forgive without receiving forgiveness first.
- We couldn't put him first without his gift of faith.
- We couldn't have faith without the Spirit opening our hearts to know Christ, who saves us.

We can't.
He can.
He does ... so we can.

Carry on.

It's Good to Have Friends in High Places

When you are invited, take the low- est place, so that when your host comes, he will say to you, "Friend, move up to a better place."
—Jesus, Luke 14:10

Jack's in trouble. He needs your help.

—Nina Myers, on the phone with Senator Palmer

>>Within the first month of my term I will instate you in a high-level position in Washington.
—Senator Palmer on the phone to George Mason

Victor Drazen is alive and free. His son Alexis is alive—barely—in a well-guarded hospital. Jack Bauer is alive but held captive in Drazen's deadly grip.

The stakes are high. The chips are on the table. Victor Drazen wants three of a kind ... a reunion with his two sons. Jack wants a full house ... a reunion with his wife and daughter. And each knows the other won't bluff.

Jack had the upper hand, and it was curled and in Victor Drazen's face. But the crushing blow never happened.

> **"Victor Drazen wants three of a kind ... Jack wants a full house."**

Drazen played his hand and anticipated cashing in the chips. But the game wasn't over. Jack wouldn't fold. The Drazen clan needed a Jack. He'd serve as a bargaining chip. An Alexis Drazen for a Jack Bauer. Straight up. The game wasn't over after all. But now Drazen had the upper hand.

Time to cash in. Call in the big guns. Bauer's silent partner will play one hand for Jack. She calls for one card—a soon-to-be-presidential power play. She knows it hasn't been played yet.

"Senator, thank you for taking my call."

"What can I do for you, Ms. Myers?"

"Jack's in trouble. He needs your help."

The game isn't over yet. Jack would give his life for a full house. He won't fold until he gets it. And a powerful friend takes his side.

Yes, Jack, it's nice to have friends in high places. In the last several hours, having the Senator on your side has proven beneficial. This time Palmer gets the ball rolling by offering Mason a high-level office when Palmer becomes president.

Mason bites at the tempting offer faster than Eve can say, "The Devil made me do it!" He goes against CTU headquarters and gives the okay. Mason accepts the offer of someone higher up than his higher-ups.

> **"Mason bites at the tempting offer faster than Eve can say, 'The Devil made me do it!'"**

Not surprisingly, Jack gets another chance to live. But he owes his life to his friend in a high place. Where would he be without his personal savior, Senator Palmer?

Hey, do I detect a faith truth staring me in the face if I make a few minor changes in that paragraph?

Sure! Not surprisingly, *we* get another chance to live. *We* owe *our* lives to *our* friend in a high place. Where would we be without our personal Savior, Jesus Christ? I don't know about you, but I don't want to think about where I'd be without him. That's one scary thought!

>>IT LOOKS LIKE WE HAVE A FAITH TRUTH STARING US IN THE FACE.

I've been trying to remember if I have any friends in high places. I do have a friend who worked on the fourth floor (I guess that's not really very high), but now he's back on the ground floor, thanks to downsizing. So I guess having friends in high places doesn't guarantee they'll always be in high places, at least according to the world's standards.

"Do you have friends in high places?"

I don't see myself calling on the few people I do know who might be in positions of influence. I've never called them out of the blue just to jaw with them. How 'bout you? Do you have friends in high places? (If so, would you mind introducing them to me?) Seriously, if so, have you called on them when you needed something? How often do you call or stop by their places just to talk? And if you do call on them, how do they respond to your request—happy to oblige, put you off, or make you feel guilty?

>> TOO OFTEN WE USE HIM LIKE A GENIE IN A BOTTLE, OR IN THIS CASE, A JESUS IN A BOTTLE.

If you think about it, you have a friend in the highest of places. Your and my ultimate Friend makes himself available at all times and in all places. This friend encourages us to call on him day and night, round the clock—not the usual request made by influential allies, is it? Unfortunately though, it's easy to wait until we've run out of any other options to call in the divine cavalry. Too often we use him like a genie in a bottle, or in this case, a Jesus in a bottle.

"He wants to unleash it on us and on our lives of faith."

We have to get it into our heads—and more important, our hearts—that this friend can do the impossible (see Luke 1:37). Although in *24*, the handful of concessions Senator Palmer arranges so quickly for Jack seems almost impossible—or improbable, at the least—our Friend has more power in his nail-scarred right hand than all the political leaders who ever lived combined! And he wants to unleash heaven's power, grace, life-changing forgiveness, joy, and more. He wants to unleash it on us and on our lives of faith. It's right there.

"God handpicked a wheat thresher."

So often though, we choose not to play the grace-powered hand he deals us. If it would be possible for Jesus to go crazy, we'd probably drive him there. Thankfully, he's patient and filled with love for us.

>> **AT FIRST GLANCE YOU MIGHT THINK *OPHRAH* MEANS "WEALTHY WOMAN." BUT IT DOESN'T. THAT'S OPRAH. *OPHRAH* ACTUALLY MEANS "DUST."**

A component of that incredible truth is that the Lord often unleashes his gifts even when we don't ask for them. You've experienced that, I'm sure. I know I have. So has Gideon. He's got a great testimony.

Gideon lived in a tough time during the history of God's people. For a seven-year stretch, the Israelites had turned so far away from God, they were subjected to the rule of the Midianites. Then God chose a leader to go up against the Midianites. Did he go with the Jack Bauer prototype? Or one with influence like David Palmer? How about

"The Lord is with you, mighty warrior."
—Judges 6:12

a warrior with the quiet strength of a Tony Almeida? No. No. And no again.

God handpicked a wheat thresher. Yes, you read that correctly, a wheat thresher. God chose someone who didn't come from a powerful family in a big city. In fact, his chosen one came from the town of Ophrah. Oh, it gets better. At first glance you might think *Ophrah* means "wealthy woman." But it doesn't. That's Oprah. *Ophrah* actually means "dust." This dust-laden wheat thresher, chosen to take on the Midianites, went by the name Gideon. Did I mention he had the confidence of a tick with dog-dander allergies?

> **"Gideon sets apart 300 doglike water-lapper-uppers."**

One day as this thresher threshes his wheat, the angel of the Lord pays him a visit and announces, "The LORD is with you, mighty warrior" (Judg. 6:12). Mighty warrior? This title seems to go in one of his dusty ears and out the other, and Gideon responds with whiny complaints about the Lord forgetting them (because he lived during such horrible times). The Lord responds by commissioning him to take care of the Midianites. So Gideon throws out excuses about being from a dusty little town and maybe mentions having the confidence of a tick with dog-dander allergies, but I'm not sure. Anyway, the Lord doesn't give up, and Gideon gives in.

Then it gets even more interesting. Gideon somehow gathers 32,000 men to attack the Midianites. The Lord says that's way too many. So 22,000 of them head back home in time for wine, cheese, and matzo appetizers. The Lord insists 10,000 is still too many. God decides to help Gideon decide who goes and who stays, telling Gideon to take them down to the water. All the men start to drink the water. The Lord tells Gideon to "separate those who lap the water with their tongues like a dog from those who kneel down to drink" (Judg. 7:5).

Who says the Lord doesn't have a sense of humor, strange as it may be?

Gideon sets apart 300 doglike water-lapper-uppers. God reassures

Gideon that he will lead these 300 men to overtake the Midianites. How is this possible? Gideon has friends in high places. He has the ultimate Friend in the high place of heaven, with whom nothing is impossible. Did you notice Gideon didn't call on him for this help—the Lord generously and of his own accord unleashed his power on this lowly wheat thresher, making him a mighty warrior.

>>HE CALLS YOU MIGHTY WARRIOR.

By the way, are you curious how many were on the roster of the opposing Midianite team? Here's the Bible's descriptive answer: "The Midianites, the Amalekites and all the other eastern peoples had settled in the valley, thick as locusts. Their camels could no more be counted than the sand on the seashore" (Judg. 7:12). That's an intimidating team to go up against.

No matter the numbers, no matter the size, no matter the number of CTU-trained camels: Gideon has the ultimate friend in high places—the Lord God. You can guess what happens next. The Friend delivers. Teaming with God, the dusty thresher boy and his band of doglike water-lapper-uppers turn the mighty Midianites away.

I'd encourage you to take the time to read the entire story of Gideon and his high-placed friend. You'll find the story in Judges 6:1–7:25. Doesn't that make you look differently at the Midianite-sized enemies waiting to attack you? It does me. Can we learn to fully trust and believe the one who makes that kind of victory possible?

Think of some supersized problems we go up against regularly:

- Midianite-sized money mix-ups
- Midianite-sized miserable memories
- Midianite-sized mean-spirited men (and women)

- Midianite-sized marriage misgivings
- Midianite-sized management mistakes
- Midianite-sized mortgage migraines

What Midianite-sized enemy looms indestructible and overpowering in your mind? Forget what your mind tells you. What does your heart say—the heart that houses the God of Gideon, the God of 300 dog-like water-lapper-uppers, and the God of your life and salvation?

He calls you mighty warrior. He arms you with mighty armor—his own. He goes with you. He gives you the victory!

When the stakes are high, and you know your enemy isn't bluffing, remember you have the winning hand, King high.

You have a friend in the highest place. You have a King *on* high who says ... "Don't fold, mighty warrior. I am on your side."

The Great Exchange on a Mountain Made out of a Molehill

He came to serve, not be served—
and then to give away his life in
exchange for the many who are
held hostage.
—Matthew 20:28 (MSG)

*Sherry Palmer boldly
instructs her husband,
"We serve a higher
purpose."
Senator Palmer
responds, "You are not
qualified to speak about
a higher purpose."*

>>I promise you, everything will be okay. It's just been a
really, really long day.

—Jack on phone to Teri

Man for man. Hostage for hostage. Good for bad. Alexis for Jack. A wounded and dying Drazen for a determined, single-minded Bauer. Even refusing to negotiate with terrorists has its exceptions ... especially when Jack Bauer sees a bigger picture, and he's been painted into the corner. The exchange is made.

In a monotone voice, Jack replies, "You want me to kill Palmer?"

>>The clock continues to tick ... as a bomb waits for detonation.

Unknowingly, Jack holds that bomb in his hand. Moments ago he held it to his ear. The explosion had to wait. Why kill one if there'll be a two-for-one special when Bauer meets with the Senator?

As if on cue, the cell phone rings. It rings twice. Three times. Four. Trying to buy time to save his daughter, Jack pleads with Palmer. Five rings. Six. *Senator, please.* Seven. *Senator, please. Answer this phone.* Eight rings. Jack hands the phone to the Senator. *Okay, Jack. I'll do what I can.* Nine rings.

This is David Palmer ... Drazen? Drazen! ...

Drazen's there. He's just savoring the moment when his revenge is realized. His finger moves downward, toward the detonation button in front of him. The two-for-one special was worth his wait.

With a near-divine revelation, Jack realizes he just handed the Senator more than a phone. In one continuous motion, Jack rips the phone from the Senator's grip, tosses it toward the patio, and tackles Palmer, shielding him with his own body just as the phone explodes and rocks the suite.

Plaster, glass, and brick shatter across the room. The floor shakes.

>>Held hostage at the port, Kim screams,
witnessing Victor Drazen pushing the button of
death.

The dust settles; everyone is shaken up. Without wasting time, Jack sees the blasted-out hole in the wall as an open door of opportunity to get his life back. Jack wants control back. Jack wants his daughter back. Jack wants his family back.

Why not let Drazen think he killed them both? Roll over and play dead. The truth doesn't leave the room; only CTU can be notified. Leak the story to the press so Drazen can hear or see for himself. Jack slips out the back door while the plan is put into motion. Jack has one thing on his mind as he races to Victor's hideout on the port—his daughter's life. Jack goes into the situation willing to give his life in exchange for the hostage named Kim.

Andre and Victor assume Kim will drown when she escapes their grip and jumps into the harbor waters. Contemplating their next move, Andre takes a call from one of his sources, Yelena, who informs him Senator Palmer isn't dead, "It was a trick to make you believe. To keep the girl alive."

Yelena hangs up while Mason and Tony discuss strategy in the next room, unaware that another mole has crawled into the building. Her name is Yelena. They call her Nina.

Exchanges splatter all over the sixty minutes of this episode:

• Alexis Drazen is exchanged for Jack Bauer.

- Andre wants to exchange Palmer's life for $2 million in frozen assets.
- After the Alexis-for-Jack exchange, the Drazens want more—Jack's life for their hostage, Kim.
- A mole at CTU exchanges the correct layout of the underground prison for an altered one.
- Sherry Palmer exchanges ethics for political power.
- Palmer exchanges his freedom, feigning a bogus death for Kim's life.

Exchanges seem in vogue today, also:

- An employee exchanges morals for money.
- A parent exchanges high standards for double standards.
- A student exchanges principles for popularity.
- An employer exchanges values for vanity.
- A Christian exchanges ethics for evil.

> **"Bad deals, senseless exchanges fill the pages of Scripture."**

We can go back to Adam and Eve to find the first unequal and ill-advised exchange—life for death, a perfect world for a sin-filled world. Bad deals, senseless exchanges fill the pages of Scripture. Who can forget the infamous exchange Judas made—Jesus' life for thirty pieces of silver (see Matt. 26:14–16)? Now there's a wise move! Godliness for greed.

Jesus also warns against a popular, yet deadly, exchange in Matthew 16:26. "What good will it be for a man if he gains the whole world, yet forfeits his soul? Or what can a man give in exchange for his soul?"

The world is at our fingertips, isn't it? There's not much distance between our fingertips and our palms. So why not wrap our fingers around it and pull it in toward our palms. Once it gets settled in our palms, we can wrap our hands around it and hold on for dear life. Actually, when we do that, life isn't so dear. As we wrap our hands around the world, our love for God is squeezed out. We can't hold on to God's gifts and promises while holding on to the world we covet. Our hands just aren't big enough for both. Something's gotta give.

> **"Now there's a wise move! Godliness for greed."**

On the other hand, wise exchanges are encouraged. For instance, our Savior exchanges our weakness for his strength. Paul sends that encouragement in 2 Corinthians 12:9–10.

> [The Lord] said to me, "My grace is sufficient for you, for my power is made perfect in weakness." Therefore I will boast all the more gladly about my weaknesses, so that Christ's power may rest on me.... For when I am weak, then I am strong.

>>OUR SAVIOR EXCHANGES OUR WEAKNESS FOR HIS STRENGTH.

Exchanges make up a good chunk of our lives. I wonder what someone would exchange for our lives? What do you think our lives are worth to someone else? While our guts might say, "Not much," our hearts might not accept that answer, asking us to reconsider. I guess that's because our Savior makes his home in our hearts, and he thinks we're mighty valuable. His personal exchange proves our worth to him.

> **❝His personal exchange proves our worth to him.❞**

[Jesus] came to serve, not be served—and then to give away his life in exchange for the many who are held hostage. (Matt. 20:28 MSG)

Hostage situations don't just make for good television drama. They make dramatic miracles in our lives lived in real time too. To better understand, let's insert our names into the verse above.

> [Jesus] came to serve, not be served—and then to give away his life in exchange for Tim Wesemann, who was held hostage.

Go ahead, and exchange my name for yours. Read it slowly. Read the love that seeps from between the lines. Steady yourself as you take in the incomprehensible exchange—Jesus gave away his life in exchange for us, hostages to sin and death. Bound and gagged, we twist and writhe, hoping to free ourselves from captivity to sin. Ahhh, but then comes the great exchange—the grace exchange.

It took place on a mountain named Calvary. You could say the great exchange took place on a mountain made out of a molehill. CTU knows about moles—dirty agents that need to be exposed. Do we know about

>>AHHH, BUT THEN COMES THE GREAT EXCHANGE—THE GRACE EXCHANGE.

moles too? Dirtied by sin, we disguise our look with perfect masks, so others won't see the mole in us. As moles, we act against the directions of our leader. We try to hide our true selves, make alliances with the enemy. We secretly try to sabotage the mission of the One we serve with venomous words and acts of insubordination. But there's One from whom we can't hide.

Could we be considered dirty agents—belonging to Christ yet still doing a lot of dishonorable deeds for the Devil? We're in desperate need of a great exchange. Jesus says he wants to take our sins and exchange them for his perfect, all-encompassing forgiveness on Calvary—a mountain made out of a molehill.

> **"We try to sabotage the mission."**

The great exchange went down outside Jerusalem's city gates. The travelers who passed by were so caught up in their lives, they didn't realize the exchange was taking place right in front of them. The world's Savior, Jesus Christ, the very son of God was pinned to a cross with Roman nails as he gasped for air to fill his lungs—air he himself created.

While people passed by, turning their backs on the blood and gore, only one back absolutely needed to be turned. When that happened and God his Father turned a back to him, Jesus cried out, not only in physical pain but in a more intense spiritual pain, *"Eloi, Eloi, lama sabachthani?"*—which means, "My God, my God, why have you forsaken me?" (Matt. 27:46). The Father turned his divine back on his Son. He had to. He had to for the great exchange to take place—to save us, to save the world.

The perfect sacrifice, the perfect exchange, wouldn't take place unless the perfect Son took all our sinful imperfections upon himself. He took our sins as well as the unspeakable wrath of the Father for those sins all upon himself. We deserved that punishment, but if it were unleashed on us, we'd never survive.

God the Father sacrificed his own Son in order to spend eternity with us. Jesus' perfect for our imperfect lives. One for one. One for each one throughout all history and the history yet to be made. His life for you. His life for me.

The exchange causes the sins that bind us, holding us hostage, to fall from our bodies and lives. He exchanges the bondage for free and grateful praise from the ones he serves, the hostages set free.

> [Jesus] came to serve, not be served—and then to give away his life *in exchange for the many who are held hostage.* (Matt. 20:28 MSG)

Let's run—we're free! The exchange worked perfectly. We're free ... free to run into his arms of mercy. We're free to run and tell the world about the great exchange that took place on a mountain made out of a molehill. We're free! Hostages no more, we're free to run.

This is the way our Savior God wants us to live.

> He wants not only us but everyone saved, you know, everyone to get to know the truth we've learned: that there's one God and only one, and one Priest-Mediator between God and us—Jesus, who offered himself in exchange for everyone held captive by sin, to set them all free. Eventually the news is going to get out. This and this only has been my appointed work: getting this news to those who have never heard of God, and explaining how it works by simple faith and plain truth. (1 Tim. 2:3–7 MSG)

"Hostages no more, we're free to run."

When It's All Said and Done, You'll Know Who You Are

>>As hard as it's been for everyone, I think this last day has been about finding out who you really are ... and not just as a candidate.
—Mike, Palmer's chief aide

Ignoring speed limits, Jack heads for the docks to complete the exchange—his life for Kim's.

You've done all this not because of who I am but because of who you are—out of your very heart!—but you've let me in on it.
—2 Samuel 7:21 (MSG)

>>I don't think you're fit to be the first lady.
—Senator Palmer to his wife, Sherry

>>Nina, I've just confirmed that someone at CTU
is feeding the Drazens information.

The phone lines are hot. News moves quickly from Jack's mouth to Andre's ear via Yelena's split, venom-spewing tongue. Victor hijacks the conversation, commanding her to falsely inform Jack that his precious daughter is dead. That news will bring Jack out of hiding.

Yelena/Nina executes the order, and the news almost executes Jack. Instead, his grief transforms into Hulk-like anger.

Jack hijacks the Drazens' van. With nothing to lose and shielding himself with the van, Jack aims the vehicle at the building, expecting it to explode on impact. Like a fireworks display, the light-enhanced glass sprays across the boathouse. Pallets fly! Crates burst on impact! Metal grinding against metal pierces the eardrum. Jack barrels out the back of the van. Guns in both hands, he sends bullets flying across Dock 11A. Andre, Victor, and Jack play out the deadly game of Terminator in real time. Looking for a clear shot at Jack, Andre makes his body a vulnerable target and Jack seizes the moment. One bullet. One corrupt heart exposed. One Drazen dead. And then there were two. Victor Drazen. Jack Bauer.

Victor skillfully hits the moving target and Jack collapses, writhing in pain, grabbing his left hip. Drazen stands over his nemesis. Victor's eyes glaze over with a layer of revenge. He proudly pulls the trigger. Click. Nothing. Click. Nothing. Victor stands defenseless.

Wounded but very much alive, Jack gets to finish the job he started years earlier—two years to the day. The Drazen patriarch stares at the barrel of Jack's gun. He's survived the last twenty-three hours waiting for this moment. He grimaces and blinks hard.

Face-to-face. Eyes locked. Gun positioned.

>>The clock is ticking ... second after second.

Jack's anger rears back, explodes through his body and releases itself through the barrel of his gun. Victor closes his eyes, and Jack opens fire ... and doesn't stop until he's emptied his gun. Twelve bullets. No doubt this time. Victor Drazen is dead, and there'll be no miraculous resurrections.

At the same time bullets fly at the dock, at CTU headquarters Nina needs only one bullet and one silencer to permanently silence her hostage.

>>The clock continues to tick ... while hearts stop beating.

Knowing Kim has been transported back to CTU from the dock, Jack speeds through town to reunite with his wife and daughter. Expectantly, Jack enters CTU headquarters. There's Kim, but where's Teri?

Jack's pulse skyrockets. A dead agent lies on the floor, and he realizes Nina turned on them all. "Teri!" No response. Next room. Nothing. Another room ... Jack screams out her name, until his voice goes silent and his pain begins to cry out. "Teri!"

Jack scoops Teri's bloodstained, limp body into his arms and holds her close. Sobbing, he holds his love in his arms. Shocked, he calls her name. Saddened, his heart empties itself.

>>Teri! No, Teri!

When all is said and done, Drazen got the last word.

>>I'm so sorry ... so sorry.

Charlotte's obituary caught my eye and my heart.

Rall, Charlotte S., 74, Collinsville, IL, Nov. 23, 2005.
No visitation or funeral service. Mrs. Rall was cremated.

>>I'D GUESS THE MAJORITY OF US
WOULD SAY NOBODY REALLY KNOWS US.

I don't know Charlotte, but I hurt for her in life and in death. Who is she? What made her smile? Who broke her heart? Did she know Jesus? When all was said and done, who was left to wonder? Who are you, Charlotte Rall?

I'd guess the majority of us would say nobody really knows us. Maybe we're untrusting. Maybe we don't want to be vulnerable. Maybe we've chosen not to allow people in.

Season One of 24 illustrates my point. Who are you—Nina or Yelena? Jamey—clean or dirty? Victor Drazen—dead or alive? Alan York or Kevin Carroll? Sherry Palmer—fit or unfit first lady? Rick—good guy or bad guy? Alexis—Elizabeth's love or deceiver? Kim—child or adult?

Senator Palmer, as your chief of staff told you, "As hard as it's been for everyone, I think this last day has been about finding out who you really are ... and not just as a candidate."

And then there's Jack, Mr. Everything. At the end of the longest day of your life, we didn't expect to describe you as a widower and a single parent. What a difference a day can make ... in finding out who you are.

> **" The pain wasn't physical; rather, it was the pain of a soul longing for home. "**

Our friend Job had a Bauer-kind-of-day. Within twenty-four hours his life completely fell apart. All ten of his children, their spouses, the servants, and the livestock were killed in one fell swoop that day.

So, at the end of the longest day of his life, he let out one very long verbal attack on the God who allowed it all to happen, right? Wrong! Instead, he placed his faith in the Lord of heaven and earth and even through his grief said, "The LORD gave and the LORD has taken away; may the name of the Lord be praised" (Job 1:21). That has to make someone's top ten list of the most incredible statements of faith ever spoken.

The impact that day had on his life is unfathomable. His grief incomprehensible. But we also must note ... his faith is unbending. When all was said and done that day, Job praised God. He praised God through tears and heartache and mourning. When it was all said and done, Job knew who he was—a dearly loved child of the living and res-urrecting God (see Job 19:25–26).

When all was said and done in Norman's earthly life, he knew who he was. Norman was a man from the congregation where I served as pastor. I witnessed him writhe in pain for an hour and a half. The pain wasn't physical; rather, it was the pain of a soul longing for home. As

>>ARE YOU BEGINNING TO KNOW WHO YOU ARE—REALLY ARE?

his lungs struggled to take in enough air during those final ninety minutes of his life, he cried out over and over, "Take me home, Jesus. Please! Take me home!" He longed for home like I've never witnessed before. Norman knew he was a dearly loved, forgiven child of God. He knew he didn't deserve that title. Nor do we.

Our Savior has brought us to this moment in our day and in our lives. His Word not only reveals who Jesus is, but who we have become because of him. Are you beginning to know who you are—really are?

I'm so glad my friend Dave Moellenhoff knew he was a child of God through faith in Jesus Christ. He knew that he was dearly loved, he was forgiven, and he was saved. He knew and trusted that truth for thirty-eight years ... even on December 15, 2001. That's when Dave made it home. It was likely the longest day of his family's lives, but it was the beginning of Dave's longest day that would have no end.

Matt Quick, Dave's brother-in-law, wrote a prayer, shared at the funeral. Here are a few lines from the prayer, which may help you as you process your own longest days.

> **"Dry up the cold rain of grief with the warm light of your grace and the strong wind of your Spirit."**

Holy Father...

We bow today, overwhelmed and exhausted by the hard rain of grief that has drenched us over the past four days. We huddle together, humbled by the fragileness of life and haunted by the reality of heaven. This gentle giant, who we knew so well, now so suddenly resides there; greeting old friends, exploring the home you carefully prepared, running like the wind and staring into your face. Our voices are hoarse from screaming, "Why? Why Dave? Why now?" Thank you for the freedom to question and for being big enough and kind enough to absorb our pounding while holding us in your strong embrace. How you hate death, having endured the crucifixion of your own Son to take away its sting. Sometime, at the right time, this world will pass away and death with it and all our questions will be answered. Give us the grace and courage and patience to wait until that day ...

Grafted in you, Dave was a branch that bore abundant fruit. The river of life flowed out of your heart, coursed through his character, and spilled out on us. Dry up the cold rain of grief with the warm light of your grace and the strong wind of your Spirit. Cause that seed to grow, that the best part of Dave, those qualities of your character, might be borne in us.

>>The clock is ticking ...

When all was said and done, my friend Dave knew who he was—a forgiven, saved, and dearly loved child of the Son of God.

>>The clock is ticking ...

When all is said and done with this book, this day, this life ... I pray you confidently know you are his. Let him wrap you in his grace-saturated truth of love as you find safety and life in the arms of Jesus.

This is not the end ... our God is a God of the living!

>>His heart is beating ...

>>for you!

Notes

Faith Truth #3

1. George Sweeting, *Who Said That?* (Chicago: Moody Press, 1994, 1995), 325.

Faith Truth #4

1. Sweeting, *Who Said That?*, 190.
2. Martin Marty, *Places Along the Way: Meditations on the Journey of Faith* (Minneapolis: Augsburg Fortress, 1994), 28.

Faith Truth #5

1. Nathan Lawrence, *Far Away* CD, 2004 Mike and Nathan LCC. Used with permission.

Faith Truth #8

1. Donald Miller, *Blue Like Jazz* (Nashville: Thomas Nelson, 2003), 33–34. (Text summarized by Tim Wesemann.)

Faith Truth #11

1. Lawrence, *Far Away* CD.

Faith Truth #13

1. David Edwards, *Has God Given Up on Me?* (Colorado Springs: Cook Communications Ministries, 2004), 80.

Faith Truth #17

1. Søren Kierkegaard, *The Prayers of Kierkegaard,* ed. Perry LeFevre (Chicago: University of Chicago Press, 1956), 147, quoted in John Ortberg, *The Life You've Always Wanted* (Grand Rapids: Zondervan, 2002), 11.

Readers' Guide
FOR PERSONAL REFLECTION AND GROUP DISCUSSION

Jack Bauer's Having a Bad Day

AN UNAUTHORIZED INVESTIGATION OF FAITH IN
24: SEASON ONE

Jack Bauer can wear a person out. So can life in real time. Jack Bauer's adrenaline-charged, nonstop life captivates viewers all over the world. Christ's grace-charged, nothing-can-stop-him life wants to captivate hearts all over the world as well. His life in real time ... time without end.

It's exhilarating to see God and his God-work in every aspect of life. Thankfully, we don't have to wait week to week to observe our Lord's handiwork. He constantly presents us with faith truths around every corner of our lives—even during the longest days of our lives. Through the Spirit, we begin to see God-created life-bridges in every situation and conversation we enter—and even as we sit down to watch the longest day of Jack Bauer's life unfold.

The following study guide provides discussion questions designed for use in your personal devotions, in a Bible study group, or in a discussion among friends. Anyone can use this book or guide—24 fan or not. We pray this guide—and the book—will spark more discussion and deeper digging into Scripture. However you choose to use this study guide, remember to make room for an additional guest—the Holy Spirit, who works through God's Word, strengthening and energizing faith.

Abundant blessings as God grows your faith!

Yes, the clock is ticking.

But more important, the heart of Jesus is ticking ... for you!

FAITH TRUTH #1
Life on the Run Isn't a Walk in the Park

1. Sneaking out of the house, Kim and Janet attempt to run from childhood into adulthood. How much of your life have you spent "on the run" from something or someone?

2. Kim chose an Internet password that describes her feelings about life. What passwords would you make up to describe your life at various ages?

3. Read and discuss 1 Kings 19:1–18. How do the various situations in this portion of Elijah's life resonate in your life? How did the Lord respond to Elijah?

4. Without naming names, how many people in your life could easily say with Elijah, "I have had enough, Lord" (1 Kings 19:4)? How can or have you helped?

5. When are times Jesus and/or his disciples seemed to live "on the run"? How did they get through those times?

FAITH TRUTH #2
Trust Is a Must

1. What trust issues do you struggle with in your daily life and in your life of faith?

2. We so easily blame God during difficulties. Why is it so easy? How does God show himself faithful, trustworthy, and loving even during those tough times?

3. If you've been betrayed by a family member or friend, what was your response? How did Jesus respond?

4. Discuss Tim's statement, "Trust in Jesus Christ is a must for healthy, joyful living." With God's help, how can you reflect a healthy, joyful life?

5. What Bible verse or story shines as a strengthening example as you strive to place your trust in God?

FAITH TRUTH #3
Self-Serve Lines Serve Little Purpose

1. In the last week, how and in what situations did you practice "self-rescue," ignoring God's help?

2. Were you taught to pull yourself up by your own bootstraps?

3. How has your view of serving changed as your faith has grown?

4. Discuss the place of Luke 12:13–21 in your life. What is Christ's good news when the principle in verses 20–21 hits us between the eyes?

5. Do you feel kidnapped by your job? family? church? school? debt? How has/does/can Jesus respond to those situations?

6. Discuss Tim's statement, "There's a line—sometimes a fine one—between greedy selfishness and healthy ambition."

As a Matter of Fact, It's a Matter of Faith

1. When you have faith issues or questions, to whom do you turn for help, a listening ear, or answers?

2. Share mountaintop and valley experiences you've had during your faith walk. How did they affect you or those around you?

3. How did God strengthen your faith in the last week or month?

4. Who serves as your faith hero or mentor?

5. In Matthew 16:15, Jesus asks, "Who do you say I am?" Over the years, how has your answer changed? What brought about the change?

There's Stability in an Unstable Environment

1. Tim writes, "My friend described [24's] average viewers as independent thinkers and adrenaline junkies." Does that describe you? Do you agree with the statement?

2. Who or what brings stability into your life (besides Jesus)?

3. Discuss Psalm 13. What changes the tone of the psalm? How does the psalm echo your faith walk?

4. Share examples regarding the stable and seemingly unstable times in Jesus' life. How does he relate to your environment?

5. How did the Christmas letter in this chapter affect you?

FAITH TRUTH #6
Deception Can Be Deceiving

1. Share times when you've been deceived and how you felt about that deception.

2. What deceptive lies of Satan have you believed?

3. Share examples of times when you've put on a mask to deceive people into believing something about you. Why is that so easy?

4. How has God's forgiveness impacted your life and any times of deception?

5. Satan is the ultimate deceiver. How often you do consider Satan's presence in your life? Mix Ephesians 6:10–18 into the discussion.

FAITH TRUTH #7
Unexpected Freedom Comes to Unsuspecting Prisoners

1. How does Isaiah 61:1–3 (especially v. 3) impact your days?

2. Don Clair says we overestimate our power and underestimate God's. How? When? Why?

3. How do events, people, and sin imprison us? Where is the prison's key located?

4. Have you felt it wasn't possible for God to love you? What freed you from that prison?

5. Discuss the prayer at the end of the chapter, then pray it, leaving time for silent naming of imprisoning sins.

FAITH TRUTH #8
Love Covers a Multitude of Fears

1. What is the meaning of 1 Peter 4:8?

2. Has your view of love ever been distorted? What about your view of God's love? Discuss how this could happen.

3. How has fear played a part in your love for God and for others?

4. How have your views of Christ's return changed over the years? Did this chapter help calm any fears?

5. What is complete and fearless love, according to 1 John 4:16–19?

FAITH TRUTH #9
There's a Genesis for Every Problem

1. What difficult situations or decisions touched your life recently? How do you usually respond to tough times?

2. Had you been taught that Job didn't ask "Why?" questions? Check out Job's questions in this book, and discuss what you observe.

3. Are there appropriate and inappropriate times to ask God, "Why?"

4. Does guilt play a big role in your life? How does God change that?

5. Can we say, "It's God's will" to every situation? Apply the statement "Sin is never God's will" to recent news stories.

FAITH TRUTH #10
A Master's Degree in Communication Speaks Volumes

1. How do you relate to the prayer in this chapter?

2. What easily distracts you when praying?

3. Discuss the truth of Romans 8:28 and it's impact on your faith.

4. What changes do you want God to help bring about in your prayer life?

5. What questions do you have about prayer? Who taught you how to pray, if anyone?

FAITH TRUTH #11
Losing Control Brings Everything Under Control

1. What does Galatians 2:20 mean? Specifically apply it to your life.

2. Why is it so hard to lose control and let God take the wheel?

3. Expound on the words, "Crucified with Christ? Crucifixion means I can't turn around—I'm facing straight ahead!"

4. What part does ego play in living Galatians 2:20?

5. Discuss the prayer at the end of this chapter.

FAITH TRUTH #12
Not Everyone Is in the Dark

1. About what have you been left in the dark this past week? Were they important matters? How did you respond?

2. Do you easily give up? Why or why not?

3. Read Luke 24:13–35. Discuss some possible reasons Jesus chose not to reveal himself to his fellow walkers earlier.

4. Have you ever felt you were living the words in Luke 24:32?

5. Share times when you felt God left you in the dark. Does he have the right to do that?

6. What's the most important truth he has revealed to you?

FAITH TRUTH #13
Claim Responsibility, Not Injustice

1. Discuss recent news stories that illustrate the fact that people find it hard to claim responsibility for their actions.

2. Galatians 6:4–5 reminds us not to be impressed with ourselves or compare ourselves to others. How does this speak to your life?

3. What is behind Pilate's words in Matthew 27:24?

4. Name other situations in the Bible where someone wouldn't claim responsibility for actions.

5. What faith truths shine from Titus 3:3–5?

FAITH TRUTH #14
Legalism Levels Lives

1. Have you been in situations that didn't allow any deviation from protocol?

2. What faith truths and teachings come from Romans 3:21–24? How do you feel about being justified (declared not guilty) by God's grace?

3. What does legalism mean to you? What part has it played in your life?

4. Is obedience to God's Word a law, a response, or both?

5. Are you familiar with the truth of James 2:10? What do these words say to you? How do they apply to your walk with Jesus?

FAITH TRUTH #15
Compassion Makes for a Great Passion

1. What great acts of compassion have others shown to you?

2. In what ways has the world's expression of compassion changed over the years?

3. What does Matthew 9:36 tell us about Jesus? About the crowds that followed him?

4. When have you been surprised that a person cared about you?

5. How has God's gift of forgiveness impacted and changed your life and your ability to forgive?

FAITH TRUTH #16
Chinks in the Link Have Different Meanings

1. When have you felt like the weak link? What brought on that feeling?

2. How do our sins affect our link with Jesus?

3. Thumbing through 1 and 2 Kings, what tells you that life is all about the relationship with the King?

4. What's the only way we'll hear Jesus say to us, "My child, you did what is right in my eyes"?

5. Pray the prayer at the end of the chapter, pausing for personal reflection after each sentence.

FAITH TRUTH #17
Mirrors Don't Tell the Whole Story

1. Fess up! What don't you like about what a mirror shows you? Why do you use mirrors? Do they tell your whole story?

2. What does 1 Corinthians 13:12 mean? Why is it part of the "love chapter"?

3. How did the teaching about Matthew and Simon the Zealot in this chapter shape your thinking about Jesus, his disciples, and the power of his presence?

4. Discuss Kierkegaard's prayer, "And now, Lord, with your help I shall become myself."

5. Read 2 Corinthians 3:4–5, 17–18. How are we transformed into Christ's image?

FAITH TRUTH #18
Remembering to Forget Creates Unforgettable Memories

1. Is it difficult to trust God's promise to forgive and forget our sins?

2. When were you first taught Jesus remembers to forget our forgiven sins?

3. This past week, how often could you have used a delete key for your words or actions?

4. How can you more easily remember to forget when it comes to forgiving others?

5. As humans, we can't perfectly forget our sins or someone's sin against us. What does it mean then when we are called to "forgive and forget"?

FAITH TRUTH #19
Dull Doesn't Describe Our Lives

1. What's the craziest thing you've ever done? How did it make you feel?

2. Using the list of movie titles in this chapter, which best describes your life ... today, last year, five years ago?

3. The ad reads, "We'll sell you the whole seat, but you'll only need the edge!" When (if ever) have you felt that way in Bible study, worship, prayer, or just living in God's presence?

4. What affects the atmosphere of your life—makes it good or bad?

5. How important is rest (physical and spiritual) to you? How would others answer that about you?

FAITH TRUTH #20
The Lion Doesn't Sleep Tonight

1. How has your view of Satan changed over the years?

2. Discuss the meaning of Ephesians 4:27.

3. How does 1 Peter 5:8 affect the way you live?

4. Give examples of how a temptation starts innocently but ends disastrously.

5. What were your thoughts regarding the "Five-Chapter Book" in this chapter?

FAITH TRUTH #21
You Didn't Get There by Yourself

1. Share recent situations when you didn't get "there" by yourself.

2. How does John 15:5 shape the view of yourself?

3. Mark 2:1–12 shares a visual story and deep truths. Put yourself in one of the various characters' roles in the story. How does that change your perspective?

4. Why is it so easy to forget that forgiveness is a miracle? How can that truth change our view of forgiveness?

5. Who helped carry you to Jesus?

FAITH TRUTH #22
It's Good to Have Friends in High Places

1. When have you used someone's position in life for your own good?

2. Read John 15:15. What does it mean to you to know Jesus considers us, his disciples, friends?

3. Share examples of times in your life when the Lord, on his own accord, unleashed his power and grace.

4. How do you see yourself in Gideon's life and story (Judg. 6–7)? Explain.

5. Tim wrote about Midianite-sized problems in our lives. What are some large obstacles you deal with daily or are dealing with now?

FAITH TRUTH #23
The Great Exchange on a Mountain Made out of a Molehill

1. If a ransom was placed on your life, how much would you be worth ... to your family, to your coworkers, and to your God?

2. Have you ever felt like you were being held hostage by a sin or a sin-filled situation? Describe your feelings.

3. Tim writes that exchanges seem in vogue today. What does he mean by that? What are some examples?

4. Read Matthew 16:26. Have you observed this situation in the lives around you? Has this been a struggle for you?

5. What exactly was exchanged through Jesus' death and resurrection? Are you able to still stand in awe of that exchange?

FAITH TRUTH #24
When It's All Said and Done, You'll Know Who You Are

1. Tim suggests that the majority of us would say nobody really knows us. Do you agree? If so, why is that? Would you say nobody really knows you (besides our all-knowing God)?

2. What does it mean to claim that your identity is in Christ?

3. When your life is said and done, what will be the most important words said about you and the most important action done on your behalf?

4. What are your concerns, fears, and joys about living eternally in heaven? Have you shared them with your family or friends? How do the promises of Jesus influence those thoughts?

5. Who are you? How might others describe you? How might God describe you?

About the Author

Tim Wesemann is founder of Foolish Words (1 Cor. 1:18), a ministry of writing and speaking. His writing includes twenty-two books with more than 500,000 copies in print, including translations in Chinese and French. Tim's full-time ministry of writing began in 2000, after he served as a pastor for the previous eleven years. Besides books, Tim's published work includes greeting cards, dramas, booklets, pastoral aids, music lyrics, devotionals, magazine articles, and curriculum. Tim and his family live in St. Louis. Learn more at www.FoolishWords.com.

Additional copies of *Jack Bauer's Having a Bad Day*
are available wherever good books are sold.

If you have enjoyed this book, or if it has had an impact on your life,
we would like to hear from you.

Please contact us at:

LIFE JOURNEY BOOKS
Cook Communications Ministries, Dept. 201
4050 Lee Vance View
Colorado Springs, CO 80918

Or visit our Web site:
www.cookministries.com

LIFE JOURNEY®
Bringing Home the Message for Life